Free Your Mind

It's Not What
You Think

Free Your Mind

It's Not What
You Think

Steven Pashko

Fluidity
P. O. Box 627
Lansdale, PA 19446
www.StevenPashko.com
Tel: (215) 880-5169

Cover and interior design by Joan Greenblatt

Printed in the United States of America

ISBN: 0-9745498-0-0

Library of Congress Catalog Card Number: 2004095469

"*Problems cannot be
solved with the same
consciousness that
created them.*"
—Albert Einstein

TABLE OF CONTENTS

ACKNOWLEDGEMENTS

I CAN'T take much credit for writing this book. Although it took many years of preparation, this book was an effortless effort. It simply came through my wish to help those, including myself, who have struggled with that harmful form of worry that I define as thought streaming.

This page, though, is where I can thank all those who helped me with this writing project. I would like to express my deepest gratitude to all who directly or indirectly contributed to the book, as well as to those who encouraged me to write it. Many have contributed, and none is at fault for errors except me.

I especially would like to thank Lee Milton for all his encouragement to "just stay with it" through all these years. Good advice, indeed!

I would also like to thank those whom I have read or heard speak and who indirectly contributed to this book through their wisdom, such as Julius Axlerod, Yogi Berra, Joseph Campbell, Noam Chomsky, Steven Covey, W. Edwards Deming, Howard Gardner, Steven Gray, Carl Jung, Robert Jackman, Jeffrey Kagel, Maruti Kampli, Bob Lee, Nicolee Miller-McMahon, Ronald S. Miller, Lee Milton (again), Harvey Penick, V.S. Ramachandran, Carl Rogers, Jelaluddin Rumi, Charles Tart, Wayne Teasdale, Wolfgang Vogel, John Welwood, and Stephen Wolinsky.

Those who directly contributed to the physical development of the book include Charles (Andy) Andrews, Greg Godek, Joan Greenblatt, Matthew Greenblatt, Ronald S. Miller, Sonia Nordenson, and Chris Witt. Other indirect contributors were neuroscientists, philosophers, poets, psychotherapists, and spiritual leaders who influenced me over the years. Jennifer Nelson took the photograph that appears on the back cover.

To my friend, Charles (Andy) Andrews,
my sister, Sue Pashko,
and all who seek to free their minds from
runaway thought streams.

DISCLAIMER

While this book helps people better understand their own thought processes, it does not replace good mental health care. If such care is needed, I urge people to seek out professional sources.

As with all books dealing with mental processes, you should apply the techniques and practices suggested here earnestly and carefully. You need to be earnest to benefit from the practices. You also need to be careful in noticing your own thoughts and breaking away from them if they seem unusually disturbing.

Although they are subtle, thought streams profoundly influence our lives. We often behave according to our worried thoughts, regardless of the potential for harm in this. Thought streams can also cause behavior that is troubling. This book will help readers see through harmful and unnecessary thought streams, develop stronger mental "muscles" to discard them, and eliminate their negative effects. I don't suggest you practice any exercises described in the book in places or situations that could cause harm to yourself or others, such as when you are driving or making important financial decisions.

Noticing thought streams that you didn't notice before may cause you some concern, especially if the thoughts are antagonistic to yourself or others. Yet bringing out such thoughts for reflection and release is part of a natural healing process. If you pay increased attention to your thoughts, and the practice of dropping one thought stream after another causes you concern, please contact a mental health professional for personal care.

One final note: although the people and situations in this book are real, I have changed names and facts to protect the confidentiality of those involved.

INTRODUCTION

"Happiness depends on ourselves."
—ARISTOTLE

W H E N I was in my thirties, I went through a series of difficult learning experiences. At one time I had serious relationship problems, at other times I lost jobs, while later on there was a death in the family. Somehow each of these events caused me a great deal of suffering. I imagine that the life experience of my readers has been similar, since unfortunate events happen to us all. As the old saying goes, "Into each life a little rain must fall."

During those challenging times, most of my days were filled with sad or anxious thoughts. My mind would jump from one topic to another: from self-recrimination about disappointing my family to questions about whether there's a graceful way to end a loving relationship or how one goes about keeping a good job with a difficult boss.

I use a special term for this type of "thinking": thought streaming. When we thought stream, we allow our thoughts to ramble on unchecked, believing them to have value. In my own case, worries about various problems would drone on and on. When I was driving my car, gloomy thoughts would be right there with me. When I sat in class or at my desk at work, the same old thoughts were there. Even during meals, these thoughts continued to intrude.

These thoughts often entirely dominated my thinking. All in all, my angry, sad, and fearful thoughts gave me no respite during every moment of my waking life. As the weight of these unhappy thoughts increased, the weeks and months dragged on more slowly.

Once, while I was going through some unusually strong grief, a physician took my plight so seriously that he prescribed an anti-anxiety drug for me. But I found that only high doses of the drug really worked, and then only because it made me sleepy. The drugs just weren't effective for the problems I had.

To my good fortune, years after I was in the midst of these unfortunate experiences, I eventually decided to do a bit of book learning about anxiety. What prompted this research was my concern that the dread, sadness, and frustration I had undergone might recur later in my life. I wanted to do all I could to prevent that, since the life experiences I lived through, although fairly common to us all, had such particularly miserable mental and emotional aftereffects.

Some of the theoretical writings about anxiety that I came across in psychology were quite interesting, but unfortunately, I found little practical help. I did, however, find a great deal of help through increasing my attentiveness to the things happening around me and through choosing, out of my own volition, not to become overly interested in thoughts themselves.

MY GREATEST PERSONAL ACCOMPLISHMENT
I consider the cessation of virtually all my own thought streaming to be my life's greatest accomplishment. I've experienced two lives—

before and after the stopping of thought streams—and they've been remarkably different. I truly appreciate the unease, waste of time and energy, as well as the pure misery brought on by streaming thoughts now that they're gone.

In fact, I now see that my *thoughts themselves* contributed enormously to every problem I used to encounter. Even though I continue to receive my share of life's misfortunes, I experience my current existence as being remarkably easier and more fulfilling than my earlier life.

Once thought streams stopped intruding into my daily existence, I regained the ability to concentrate. I can now pay attention to the really important matters of life. I can truly smell and enjoy food, hear what a loved one is trying to tell me, and see beauty everywhere. I used to believe I enjoyed all those things, but I was mistaken, and the saddest part was that I didn't even know it.

Missing One's Own Life

I'm glad you've found this book. I felt impelled to write it because I was sure that readers have had experiences just like mine and have suffered needlessly just as I did.

For example, have you ever noticed that while you're eating, your mind is off examining one problem or another? While you're talking to a loved one, how often is your mind split between that person and some consideration regarding, say, your finances? And when you sit gazing at the ocean, aren't you subject to a lot of distracting thoughts about your life circumstances?

When this is your mental state—and for most people it's the nearly universal mental condition—you're actually missing your life. Your thoughts are getting between you and the experience of everyday reality.

Yet this can all change. Today, when I sit at the ocean, talk with a loved one, or enjoy a meal, there's no monologue going on inside my head. I'm just sitting and watching, listening, or eating. I experience appreciation for life circumstances both large and small, as well as full engagement in whatever is currently happening.

This is no prideful boast, but simply an honest fact. I know how I was before I started my practice of breaking away from all thought streaming. I was like 99.9 percent of the population: struggling to make sense of all the things I thought about. And as I've said, I experienced some especially unsatisfactory times. If you can imagine a "life dissatisfaction scale" ranging from 1 to 10, for me the months surrounding the most difficult events would have hovered at a score of 9. It took that much unhappiness to motivate me to look at thoughts and the pain they bring.

Now, however, I know that *all* unchecked streams of thought cause unhappiness. If you sum up your own dissatisfaction with life and arrive at a score of more than 2, real help is available to make your life happier. I've written this book because I see nearly everyone suffering with his or her own thoughts as I once did. Now that I know relief is available, I want to let others know that all thought streams can be voluntarily controlled by means of an easy and continuous practice that I call "stopping." It involves letting thoughts go and releasing them, not encouraging them when they start, and breaking free of them each and every time they get going. While the practice doesn't offer immediate relief, it does offer incremental relief as you keep practicing. If you practice long enough, you'll have complete relief from your thought streams.

With continued practice, you'll not only experience less chronic dissatisfaction with life, but you'll discover that life without thought streams becomes simple, mentally easy and joyous. As your mind becomes more open and relaxed yet focused, you'll find yourself enjoying each moment. Most of all, you'll reestablish the link to your basic sense of aliveness and enjoy the peace of a clear mind unclouded by uncontrolled streams of thought.

CHAPTER ONE

Fundamentals of Thought Streaming

"Sweep away the clutter of things that complicate our lives."
—Henry David Thoreau

T H O U G H T streams, the rambling, unchecked thoughts that dominate our minds from morning to night, plague most of us. We take this mental cacophony to be "normal," believing we must remain helpless victims of whatever mental intruders pop into awareness. However, I've found that when thought streaming has stopped or ceased intruding into consciousness, we can avoid the needless anxiety, fear, and anger that otherwise subverts our sense of happiness. Do you have anxious, fearful, or uneasy feelings for extended periods of time? If you do, these feelings *must* be linked to some thought stream that's reactivating them over and over again.

Under optimal circumstances, all emotions come and go in relatively short order. A feeling may naturally continue for a few hours or, at maximum, up to a full day. But for an emotion to continue for longer periods or to appear as if it's remaining constant, you *must* sustain it with thoughts. The thought streaming probably stems from circumstances that occurred when its related emotion first began to develop.

An Aquatic Metaphor

The best way I know to compare life *with* thought streaming and *without* is to think of snorkeling in a huge aquarium, like one big enough for dolphins. Picture yourself in the aquarium, next to the large water intake pipe. In this scenario, you need to pull continuously with great effort on a lever so the valve will let water into the aquarium. Pulling on this lever keeps the water (representing your consciousness clouded by thought streaming) pouring in furiously over your head; otherwise, it would drain right away. While you're underwater, you can see fish (representing individual thoughts swimming through your consciousness). Often, you're intrigued by entire schools of these fish (representing streams of thought swimming through your consciousness). As they swim by, they show their fascinating colors and patterns.

You pay a price for being in the water to see the individual fish and schools of fish. Unwittingly, you use a tremendous amount of energy in pulling on the water lever. It's stressful and tiring, but you mistakenly believe it's a requirement of life.

In a world where thought streaming is no more, you completely relax your grip on the lever. You remember that your normal state is not one of being immersed in water, but of breathing free in the air. You cease your tiresome efforts of pulling on the lever, and you don't need to breathe through a snorkel anymore. Because the water has drained away, the fish are flopping on the bottom of the tank, nearly dead, and your view will no longer be clouded by water. You also no longer focus on the schools of fish lying on the bottom of the tank. Furthermore, you now can recognize your spouse standing only two feet away! You actually smell the nearby ocean and hear the wind. And now that you're breathing normally, you talk and otherwise communicate much more clearly. Welcome to a state of consciousness unclouded by thought streaming!

As a significant benefit from the practice of stopping thought streams, you regain the valuable moments *between* successive thoughts. I wonder if you can remember any times when you've had access to long periods of time between thoughts. Have you ever known these times to last longer than five minutes? If so, you have a frame of reference for experiences of true peace and ease.

Some people have these times when deeply engaged in reading, jogging, playing tennis, or doing some other focused activity. You might try playing a favorite sport to remember what this mental state is like. When we manage to gain substantial time between our thoughts, this permits enough emotional recovery after one thought so we can truly consider the next one with clear-headed awareness. Having sufficient time like this helps a lot in good decisionmaking. Otherwise, our thoughts are running our life—not the other way around.

SINGLE THOUGHTS VERSUS STREAMS

As I've pointed out, this book doesn't deal with the issues or content of our thoughts themselves. It deals with the plain fact that thought comes most often in an unwanted series, one after another, like a stream. We all have simple, single thoughts, for example of needing to eat or to buy a specific item at the market. These are the harmless thoughts we need to function ordinarily.

Thought streams, however, are different. Best described as mental chatter, thought streams keep our valuable attention locked on fruitless topics, focusing on trivialities instead of on more important matters. They also direct our mental activity, thereby blocking alternative solutions or points of view that might actually be helpful. In doing so, they close down our mind to possibilities.

Did you know that simply by discouraging thoughts or disengaging from them, you can eventually—and inevitably—stop them from streaming on? If you didn't know this, it's no wonder: Due to a general lack of awareness about it in our society, the art of paying attention to one's thoughts has been overlooked by our educational system. However, we can learn how to stop unwanted thoughts. In doing so, we can take a break, a mental breather, from their relentlessness pressure.

TWO TRUTHS

Although I understand the fine points of psychology, I'm not intrigued much by hidden meanings, Freudian slips, or the belief in a personal unconscious from which actions may unknowingly arise. I tend to be a pragmatist wanting to see results for myself. So I have no story to tell here about the deeper meanings of things, but I do have a truth to explain.

This truth is twofold. First, more often than not, single thoughts are unnecessary for living well. By single thoughts, I mean those that pop into your consciousness at seemingly random times, such as a thought that you need to buy milk or want to call someone before the day is out. This mental reminder system is the reason some of us believe we need our thoughts. They *seem* to serve as the necessary mental notepad of our life.

When we do end up at the store, if we really need milk, we'll buy it— whether or not we had the prior thought to do so. Although people believe otherwise, our actions don't usually originate from our thoughts, but occur independent of our thought processes.

We don't hit a tennis ball while thought streams are running through our mind, nor do we type or pull the covers up at night when we're cold because thought streaming tells us to do so. We just know what to do and then do it.

Second, all thought streaming is actually harmful and should be discontinued as quickly as possible. We mistakenly believe that repeated or continuous thoughts on any one topic, such as finances, a relationship, or a source of sadness, help us solve our problems. As we'll see in later chapters, thought streams don't solve problems; logical, clear thinking and wisdom do. Thought streams only burden our mental life with unnecessary complexities that add the weight of our worry to our misery. Can you remember a time in your life when worry actually offered a real solution?

I recently heard a terrible story of a woman who allegedly killed her children and spouse. From my point of view, thought streaming killed her family. Does that sound odd to you? Here's how I arrive at that opinion. I believe something initially happened in the family that made this woman feel hurt. The hurt could have come from any source—any family member—and it could have been either a physical injury or a psychological one.

After the hurt occurred, thought streaming took over her consciousness. That it can do so is the theme of this book. When we receive a hurt and allow ourselves to thought stream about it, no good can come of this. The woman probably felt the hurt in a specific way and became involved in thought streams that generalized it to broader circumstances:

"My family doesn't love me. They're dragging me down with family obligations, and that keeps me from being promoted at work. I think Pete hit me just to get the kids on his side of the argument. I can't let this go on. Everyone seems to be ganging up on me."

Thoughts that her family didn't love her, that they would harm her success in the future, and that they wanted to hurt her can take root and then go on ceaselessly.

Thoughts of this nature might contain some small basis of truth, yet ultimately they are all exaggerations. Like most of us, this woman hadn't learned to stop her own thought streaming. Because she hadn't, it encouraged her to focus strongly on her hurt. Her emotions gathered force because of her focus on these thoughts, her thoughts increased because of her emotionality, and finally, she believed that action had to be taken. By this point, there was little chance that the resulting actions would be either well-conceived or wise.

We can all look at our own lives to see how we have magnified small problems through this same process. For most of us, it hasn't ended in homicide—only in misery.

Now consider an alternative. Let's say that someone, perhaps your spouse, hurts you emotionally. You may have received a serious betrayal or a small insult; it doesn't matter. My point is that when you experience a personal wounding, you have a choice. Your thoughts about the harmful event can become magnified through uncontrolled thought streaming, or they can be handled more skillfully, so you stay with the reality of the situation.

What's the reality? Whether deliberate or inadvertent, someone hurt you. If you can stop the spiraling of thought streaming, you have a chance to look into the matter honestly and ask important questions.

What role did each of you play in this argument? What actually initiated it? What's the true extent of your injury? How can you respond so that both points of view (yours and your spouse's) are given their due?

Here's a more appropriate response to the woman's situation: *"Wow, that was the worst. Peter hit me. I can't believe he did that! I'll call the police and protective services to make sure that doesn't happen again. I can't let the kids believe his action was appropriate. I know I* goaded him on, though. I'm not to blame, but I sure didn't help the argument come to a helpful end. My arm hurts where he hit me, but it doesn't look like a bruise will appear. But the kids saw the whole thing. He and I both need to sit down with the kids and discuss what happened and say that we're sorry. The root of this problem is that it's difficult to balance home life and work life, given our spending habits. We all need to work on this, even the kids who often ask for too much."

The most appropriate way to solve these kinds of problems is through reflection. When we reflect, we're in a state of open awareness as we regard a problem or situation. Though we often do this, we typically misname it "thinking." However, in reflection there's no internal monologue—neither logical thinking nor thought streaming. Reflection occurs when the mind is simply attentive and concentrated, allowing us to clearly see a problem and its best solution. If, when you're washing the dishes, you're not worrying about one problem or another, consider the open and aware state of your mind. That's reflection.

Sometimes, though, when we're in a reflecting mode, a problem may appear more vague than usual. This vagueness is actually helpful because it stems from deconceptualizing the problem (thinking outside the box) so we can see it anew. Perhaps after reading a paragraph in a book or magazine, you wonder about what you just read. You look up from the material and reflect on its meaning. You may wonder whether you agree with the author's viewpoint or whether the recipe you read about would really taste good or not. We don't use logic or streams of thought as we ponder this way. Because our attention is high, we simply "consider" the meaning of what we just read.

Thought streaming typically magnifies a problem, limits the alternative solutions we're able to see, and causes a higher probability of harm to all parties concerned. It's a bad path to follow, both for us and for others. We would do better to stop all the mental chatter involved in thought streaming and simply reflect on our problems at the appropriate times.

EVERYONE CAN STOP UNWANTED THOUGHTS

When people say they're stressed or they feel as if they're going to have a nervous breakdown, they really mean that they can't get away from their thought streaming long enough to get some mental relief. Their thought streaming is running at top speed, out of control, as in the following example:

"This business deal is sure to fall through. If it fails, I'm sure to be fired. What will our family do? We can slow down our spending. We can forget the vacation. Geez, I need a vacation, too. I wonder if my co-worker Julie knows any other companies that are hiring?"

Was any of this thought streaming actually helpful in solving a problem, or was it all just useless worry? You can learn to stop thought streams like these (and they will inevitably stop), if you recognize the problem and make up your mind to stop them. It actually isn't hard to do. You just need to know that discipline will lead to their cessation, and then you actually have to practice.

The initial practice involves spending some time just noticing your thoughts. When you become aware of certain thoughts as involuntary and unwanted, you practice dropping your attention from them. It's helpful to place your attention on something else—perhaps a manual task like sweeping with a broom or washing dishes. Essentially, then, you're practicing disengaging or removing your attention from thought itself.

When we learn a new sport, we take it for granted that we'll have to put in some practice time. This practice of dropping your thought streaming is just like that. In fact, you already do it every night for that short period of time just before you drop off to sleep, using a similar mechanism to slow your thoughts and cause them to drop away enough for sleep to occur. You know you can't sleep with a racing mind.

From my own experience, as well as what others have told me about life without thought streaming, I can attest that daily life becomes simple, attentive, and mentally easy, as well as joyous. Consider your own current life. For most of us, daily life has quite a bit of turmoil. Your work, children, relationships, or other practical matters may keep you very busy.

Take a moment now to examine the quality of your mental life in the midst of all this activity. Many of our struggles are mental; a busy life typically means a busy mental life, too. Can you imagine how it would feel if all your mental struggles were to immediately subside? It's almost impossible to get a sense of that, isn't it? Our minds are so full of quick-acting thoughts that we don't seem to have options for dispensing with them. Yet, fortunately, they *can* go away.

The more you feel yourself struggling with your thoughts, the more you need to read this book. You're going to be amazed at what's possible. In fact, by the time you finish reading this book, you may already understand what I mean when I say that life without thought streaming is simple, attentive, mentally easy, and truly joyous.

Now that you know something about thought streams—what they are and how they can be controlled and stopped—you have a way out of mental agitation and anxiety. As part of your new approach to life, continually practice not encouraging or becoming engaged by thought streams. You do this every night, as I said, but you now need to practice as often as you can during the day as well.

An Ethical Challenge for All of Us: Keeping an Open Mind

In reading this book, you're being placed in an ethical dilemma, and at the same time, you're being challenged with how to live in this world. You may believe the world needs to change for the better. Why not stop any harmful thought streaming and cease your interest in having such thoughts? By doing this, you allow true open-mindedness to develop.

Such an open mind, free from preconceived notions about how things should be, will give you the mental flexibility needed to change the negative ways you feel and act. None of us can change for the better when our mind is full of opinions, presumptions, and destructive emotional tones. An open mind really is the way it sounds. Besides being ready to accommodate new ideas, such a mind remains free of unwanted thoughts. When we practice stopping thought streams, we also practice obtaining an open mind, which is exactly what's needed for living well and meeting the challenges of this complex world.

The Meaning of Mindfulness

If you believe your own thought streams are too incessant for your own good and notice they're having a negative impact on your quality of life, I encourage you to practice stopping them. Start by noticing your thoughts. Notice every one and stop those that you can. This is the meaning of mindfulness, being mentally clear and attentive. Keep doing this continuously as a regular part of your mental maintenance program. Stay alert and don't let your thought streaming tendencies go unnoticed. Keep them in full awareness. When you can, extract from your mind any and every thought stream that enters. This challenging practice will inevitably reap dividends.

As you progress, you'll gain more of those precious moments of time between successive thoughts, interims in which you'll luxuriate in mental peacefulness.

TRY THIS:

T O experience thought streaming for yourself, place your attention *on* your thoughts the next few times you're in the bath or shower or when you're handwashing dishes.

N O T IC E your thoughts. It's typically very easy. Can you look at them? If it's difficult, two things might help.

Y O U might hold a telephone handset and pretend you're listening to a friend. But instead of holding the handset at your ear, hold it at arm's length in front of your nose. Then pretend your friend is still speaking, but now consider that you're listening *at* the words instead of listening *to* the words.

I F you still have difficulty noticing your thoughts, you might say to yourself, "*And that last thought was about...,*" and then verbally speak aloud the words that just ran through your mind. Do this for a few minutes, but don't do it for too long. Until you get used to it, it can be tiring to keep looking at thought and then saying it back verbally. Do notice your thoughts again the next time you're in the bath or shower or when you're hand-washing dishes.

Y O U ' R E actually getting the chance to "speak your mind" in this exercise. You might warn others in the kitchen that they'll see you doing this a few times. We don't want them to believe you're odd. We want them to know that you're interested in exposing and understanding the thought in your mind.

CHAPTER TWO

Critical Omissions

"I am searching for that which every man seeks - peace and rest."
—Dante Alighieri

W H E N I went to college, I didn't have a strong motivation to continue my schooling to get a good job. I went just to get an education. Though all the arts and sciences were potential areas of study for me, I really considered only a limited number of academic majors. I believed that psychology would help me understand myself; I think that's why most students go into it. Because the late teenage years are times of great transition, like many others I wanted to better understand myself and learn how to live a meaningful life.

I wanted to understand all there was to know about how and why we humans exist. Life seemed quite perplexing to me. What was it all about? Was there some purpose? If there was, how could a life be well-lived? I soon believed that these questions were more philosophical than psychological. Yet for some reason, philosophy didn't interest me, perhaps because I didn't see any answers coming forth from philosophers—just more questions. For me, psychology held more of the answers I sought.

MY INTEREST IN PSYCHOLOGY

Some of the questions I had in school related to whether everyone shares the same kind of consciousness. Did I see and hear what you did, or was it different for each of us? If it was different, why was that? Should it be this way, or should we see things more similarly? What happened that we saw things differently from each other? Was it always this way, or did some change happen?

I wondered how much human consciousness differs from that of animals and plants. I wanted to know what was at the root of the senses of seeing and hearing. In addition, my questions concerned the workings of courage. I had heard stories and seen old movies about people who sacrificed their own lives for the sake of others. Like many others my age, I wanted to know what love was. Apparently, this deep feeling could cause a kind of self-sacrifice similar to courage, yet it seemed to express itself through different means.

I regarded love as occurring between individuals, in small personal moments. Yet I also thought of courage as a form of love arising in groups of people under high stress, as in the tragedies of shipwrecks or war. Furthermore, I had some interest in knowing about how language shapes our view of the world. For example, if our language didn't include the personal pronouns "he" and "she," as some other languages do not, would we view ourselves differently? Would gender bias vanish through this twist of communication? What would happen?

As a new psychology major, I happily entered a field of study in which one could ask these questions. I wondered what the answers would be. I certainly didn't know, yet I felt sure that someone did and that within a semester or two answers would appear.

THE INTEREST TURNS TO FRUSTRATION

Although I knew that psychology has to do with the mind and the mental working of humans and animals, I could find little instruction in how the mental apparatus actually works. It seemed psychology avoided looking at this topic in depth. Psychology did study nerve cells relating to vision, hearing, and logic, but the results looked like maps or circuits, and I didn't find that so interesting. There was no instruction on the origin of wisdom, information more important to me than the layout of any brain circuit. In addition, I couldn't find any classes that dealt with understanding courage and love. I did find a psycholinguistics course that explored how language concepts shape our lives, but it provided only the most obvious information.

I began feeling a sense of frustration with psychology classes, yet this problem seemed energizing, not thwarting. I wanted to know as much as I could about my unanswered questions, and I knew I was going to find out about them one way or another. But, sadly, those frustrating college psychology courses led only to frustrating Master's-level psychology courses. And, as I continued along these lines, my doctoral and post-doctoral psychology classes remained as unfulfilling as the earlier ones.

Through all those psychology courses, I did get to:

- Acknowledge interesting aspects of vision; for example, when the perceptual illusions consisting of two lines, like railroad tracks, seem to get closer together as they move farther away.
- Learn about stages of personality development and a personal sense of self through readings on the concepts of the ego, the unconscious, and the collective unconscious.
- Understand something about developmental stages of perception in children; for instance, at different ages they

can understand only certain relationships and not others.

- Physically touch the actual places in the brain associated with hearing and seeing.
- Train specific behaviors in animals by giving them food at the right time when they performed the correct action.

Although these matters were interesting to learn about, they didn't begin to address my questions, which were simpler and more fundamental. Essentially, psychology was teaching what I wasn't interested in learning. I now suspect that many beginning students will be as disappointed as I was to find that psychology doesn't understand much about the many deep mysteries that are a fundamental part of being human. Oddly, it teaches almost nothing about the typical thinking process and how we use and abuse it. I truly expected to learn this in psychology.

When I was in graduate school, only one point did come close to what I wanted to know about: the fact that obsessive thinking is linked to the performance of compulsive actions, like repetitious handwashing due to obsessive thoughts about being dirty. Psychology teaches about how we react through our behaviors, sensations and perceptions. Yet I couldn't find useful information on love, courage, consciousness, understanding—just descriptions of specific reactions under specific circumstances.

I felt increasingly frustrated. Like a gambler waiting for a big pay-off, I kept enrolling in psychology courses. I took all the experimental and clinical psychology courses offered to even the most advanced graduate students, until finally there were no more left to take.

What Psychology Leaves Out
Now that I'm fully (and to some extent overly) trained in psychology,

I admit to feeling a general sense of disappointment when I consider the work of psychology, psychiatry, and psychotherapy. Clinical psychologists have not deeply studied wisdom, thought, mind, love, and courage, and these omissions have had a significant impact on all of us. Granted, these topics are difficult to study scientifically, but we have a lower quality of life and we suffer needlessly because of this neglect.

Because the field doesn't address these issues significantly, I no longer perform traditional psychotherapeutic services. For me, psychology isn't appropriately attentive to the experiences of those either providing or receiving psychotherapy. I observe a great gulf between what people want in the way of help and what psychology and psychiatry offer. All too often, treatment methods miss the mark.

Furthermore, psychologists often don't carefully implement or monitor the administration of care. They rarely measure their results objectively, and they find inquiring into a patient's satisfaction with the care a relatively new idea. In conducting itself in this way, psychotherapy has reduced its effectiveness significantly. Because of this, many people who need psychological care don't seek it, even when they acknowledge that they could benefit by improving their mental health.

Those who have guided the direction of the field have shown less concern for the important area of thought *processes* (such as kinds of thought, repetition of the same thought, or the speed with which different thoughts come into consciousness). Instead, they have focused on the *content* of thought (for example, thoughts of one's work, mother, or finances). This approach has been detrimental to the field in general and to the population's overall quality of life.

Working in the realm of thought processes, however, I've found answers to many of those important questions I had when I first entered college, answers that I'll share with you in this book.

TWO NEGLECTED BUT CRITICAL PSYCHOLOGICAL FACTORS

Professionals in psychology either neglect or omit two important factors that I consider crucial to understanding mental functioning. Psychotherapists probably bear much of the responsibility for this neglect, since they're directly involved in improving our mental health and quality of life. First, psychologists focus on thought content rather than on thought process. Second, they don't understand that our persona or self-concept (our ego) is not a solid, stable entity, but merely a changeable representation of our preferences. I believe psychology can grow by increasing its investigations into these two areas. Let's look into each of them at some length.

THE NEGLECT OF THOUGHT PROCESSES IN FAVOR OF THOUGHT CONTENT

The first significant omission in psychotherapy involves minimizing the *process* of mental events while focusing exclusively on their *content*. When the *content* of thought is examined, we give importance to the symbolic meaning of individual thoughts. For instance, women may symbolically represent our mother, specific fearful objects may represent anxiety at being separated from our family, and our unwillingness to ask for a raise may represent our fear of confronting our father. Of course, symbolism has its place. However, as we try to understand ourselves, if we rely too heavily on analyzing the symbolic meaning of our interactions with others, we may identify many *possible* meanings but not come to any useful conclusion.

When we examine the *process* of our thought, we focus on how our thoughts occur as opposed to what's in them. For instance, our thoughts may be fast; many might stream through our mind quickly, while others might stick around and keep bothering us. When our minds are racing with nervousness before a job interview, we're aware of the speeded-up process by which thoughts assail us: *"I hope I get this job. I had bad breath this morning. What if it's back? Man, that wouldn't be good. My palms are sure sweaty. I've got to remember to wipe them on my pants just before I shake hands."*

When one thought lingers on, like chronic concern about being unable to pay the minimum on next month's credit card bill, we're focusing on the process of worry that sticks around unwanted. I strongly suggest that we re-examine our processing of thoughts to glean what we can from this area of mental activity. This subject has been neglected, yet it has much to offer us. We've been looking to the content of our thoughts for too much information, and in too much detail.

As an example that shows the difference in point of view between thought content and thought process, consider what happens when we wait a few days for the results of a cancer biopsy. A human resources recruiter I know named Paul had a biopsy done for possible prostate cancer. He worried about dying, with thought streams that went as follows: *"At 56, I'm too young to die of cancer. If it's cancerous, I hope it's slow growing, but what if it's fast growing? Should I do surgery, radiation therapy, chemotherapy, or some combination of them? I've got a talented girl who wants to go to art school, and it would break my heart and hers if she didn't give it her best effort to succeed in what she loves doing. I feel so sad for her right now. Though our finances are not in the best shape, if my family is frugal, we can make ends meet, but what if there's not enough for her school? What if our insurance won't cover the treatment I might need? I don't think my wife would be able to work right after I die because I'm sure she'd be heartbroken. It's good that we live near her family."*

The *content* of all the above thought streaming concerns dying and its effect on Paul and his family. It's content is simple because it's just about the basic emotions of fear, love, grief, and sadness. Yet we often feel these thought streams are complicated. We feel this way because we stream on about different things: ourselves, our spouse, our children, and our broken dreams. This may seem like a load of woe, but it's simply about how cancer takes its toll. We just make it seem complicated.

ANXIETY ABOUT THE FUTURE

When we examine Paul's *process* of thought, we see that it asks many "what if" questions to check on how things will evolve in some imagined future timeline. This "style" of thought processing focuses on the irresistible urge to wonder "what if." Yet Paul doesn't even know whether he has cancer. Also, many of his thoughts are "sticky" with emotionality, another aspect of the thought process. Deeply felt emotions, like love, grief, anger, and sadness, tenaciously grab at our heart-strings, keeping us fascinated with these feelings. Who of us doesn't like to look into strongly felt love? Who of us isn't fascinated by the sublime sense of grief or fear? When we remain fixated on these thoughts, we don't help our situation, but only make it worse through worry.

Finally, in terms of the thought process, the speed of Paul's thoughts is a significant factor. If Paul's few thought streams stretched out over an entire day, we might consider them slow, and they might cause him less concern. However, if they ran through his mind in one short, solid burst right when he put his head down on his pillow at night, they would make it impossible for him to fall asleep. (We probably all have had nights like this.) Furthermore, if his thought streaming were very rapid, he might even get out of bed to anxiously pace the floor, driven by his worries. Although the content of his thoughts is bothersome, their speed actually increases his anxiety. In truth, he can't do anything about his cancer; he may not even have cancer. While Paul's thought content is all about dying and its effects, his thought streams are making him nervous. Paul's thought process deals with the intensity of his emotions, his nonstop production of thought streams that use one "what if" question after another, and a high number of thoughts per minute occurring in his mind.

In some ways, examining the content of thought is like looking at the fossilized remains of one of our early human ancestors. We examine the fire pits, stone tools, bones from eaten food, and any existing beadwork from a variety of angles: carbon dating, microscopic comparison to other fossilized remains, and structural comparison to other primates and hominids. Yet when we complete the detailed examinations, we've discovered no sense of how happy our ancestor was! We analyze the dead remains—the data—yet we don't know any of the most meaningful aspects of that prehistoric life.

The same goes for the content of our thoughts. We may consider certain aspects, examining them in detail. Paul did this in our example when he considered how his possible demise might affect his wife, his daughter, and all their dreams. In this way, we may learn much about a specific problem, such as who will be affected by it, but lose touch with the process of how our mental reaction to it has occurred, the speed and intensity of our thoughts, and the incessant, fruitless, and harmful churning of "what if" conjectures.

Thoughts occur without our summoning or even wanting them.

Some occur repetitively. Certain seemingly trivial ones, like thoughts of being dirty, can have such force that they tear our life apart when they actually develop into obsessive-compulsive disorder. We need to look more closely at our thought patterns themselves and learn to free ourselves from the negative effects of our thought streams.

If we want to better understand obsessive-compulsive disorder and related conditions, we might focus more on a thought pattern's repetitiveness, emotional tone, and style. Noticing that I have dirty hands—the content of a situation—is qualitatively different from dealing with frequent, intense, and unwanted thoughts of dirtiness— the process of the situation.

I believe the lack of interest in thought processes among psychologists has occurred for a wide variety of reasons. Perhaps the psychologist's desire to please the patient has contributed to this problem. (We also see this behavior in physicians who inappropriately prescribe antibiotics to patients with colds.) Also, thanks to Sigmund Freud, psychotherapists have traditionally concerned themselves with thought content and may have an unconscious fear of losing their professional identity if they seriously investigated the process of thought itself.

For these and other reasons, psychotherapy has failed to reach its full potential in helping people find a higher quality of life. Some professionals may even have considered examining thought processes more closely for their therapeutic usefulness but may not have had the means to carry their investigations forward.

It will take a good deal of effort to shift psychotherapy from its exclusive focus on content to an examination of the process of thought as well. The size and scope of the omission have been great, yet the time is ripe for this change.

As part of the needed shift, psychotherapists might codify

thought streaming for clinical diagnosis. This new approach would help therapists see that many patients who complain of anxiety and depressive disorders might actually be better diagnosed as having uncontrolled thought streaming. Although the content of their thoughts might relate to anxiety or depression, the symptoms might be secondary to the harm caused by the thought streaming itself. I believe it's time to examine the impact that thought streaming has on all clinically significant mental disorders.

THE FAILURE TO VIEW THE SELF-CONCEPT AS A THE SUM OF OUR PREFERENCES

The second of the two significant omissions in psychology relates to the self-concept, or ego. My dictionary and many professionals define the ego as the mental structure that serves as the organized conscious mediator between a person and reality.

When speaking of the ego, or self-concept, some professionals (and thus patients) imbue it with real physical attributes, as if it's a solid object like a one-dollar bill. Psychotherapists may fail to remind patients that it is not a neuroanatomical structure of the brain like the hippocampus or corpus callosum. These are actual physical brain structures, which the ego is not. Mental structures such as the id and the ego are concepts, characterizations, representations, or beliefs that we use to aid us in understanding the workings of the mind. The ego is more like a verb than a noun. It is ever changeable, not fixed and solid, as many want to believe.

Like Michelangelo's painting of the *Creation of Adam* in the Sistine Chapel and Dante's narrative description of hell in *The Divine Comedy*, which are, of course not true "creation" or true "hell," mental constructs such as the ego are also simply representations. We will never find a real object called an ego, which is merely a term we use to indicate a *grasping at a memory of the sum total of what a person has come to prefer.* Some people prefer to be respected, some prefer to be loved, while others prefer not to become involved in many interpersonal relationships. We may call these people authoritarian, loving, or shy, but these are only characteristics, not the solid, sum total of their being.

An ego reflects a memory of preferences, but it isn't an object. It's a believing. At some level, we know depictions of heaven and hell aren't real. Yet we see them so often that they take on an appearance of truth. It then becomes hard to remind ourselves that these are only representations and not the real thing.

In this vein, Pope John Paul VI recently had to remind the faithful that heaven and hell are not physical locations. He needed to do so because people had seen so many paintings of these two realms that they had begun to believe the pictures were of real physical locations. In making this statement, the pope gave us all an opportunity to come to terms with our own penchant for the solidification of concepts. We normally seek to solidify any conceptual representation, be it heaven, hell, the ego, or any other. Although we all do this, it has significant drawbacks.

In clarification, let's remember that the ego is merely a grasping at a memory of the sum of our accumulated preferences. For example, I like tennis, the ocean, jeans, and silver cars. These preferences don't define me, but they express my unique preferences. If I happen to purchase a car whose color is different than silver, this doesn't change the basics of who I am. Yet some individuals take their preferences quite seriously, as if they were personally defining themselves through them.

We say that some people have a *strong ego.* This means they get angry when a preference of theirs, which has grown into a rule, has been "violated." For instance, if someone uses a racquetball racquet on a tennis court, a person with a "strong ego" might get angry at this apparent lack of etiquette. In such a case, the rule that "only tennis racquets can be used on a tennis court" may have grown from this person's simple preference into a strongly held rule. Yet even this person might have played on a tennis court with a racquetball racquet as a child when he first started learning the game. How easily we turn our simple preferences into rigid truths that must be obeyed!

Let's look now at "big egos." We hear about this phenomenon when a popular star in our culture shows great insistence regarding some preference that he's turned into a rule. For example, he *must* have his rare champagne chilled and ready for drinking after finishing a performance. We say that this individual's ego is "big" because he has an inflated sense of self-worth. His preference may have started as a simple desire to be treated well, which is something that we all want. Yet as his preference became solidified, the rule developed that this individual *must* be treated as if he is more special and important than others. When it turns into a rule, a preference loses its inherent flexibility. Earlier in his career, when he wasn't a popular star, he may have thanked anyone who offered him a glass of tap water when he got off stage. Taking advantage of his increasing star status for personal gain, he may have asked for a soft drink instead of tap water, and then asked for champagne instead of a soft drink. Finally, although he simply prefers to wet and cool his throat after a performance, he solidified the rule that he must have his rare champagne after a performance. This all-too-common problem occurs not just in show business, but in all walks of life.

The point I'm making with these examples is that many psychotherapy professionals have allowed their patients to solidify the ego into a seemingly real structure. With both the professional and the patient buying into this solidification process, the work of psychotherapy changes from a potentially life-enhancing process to one of patching injured and supposedly solid egos back into consistency with their preference systems. But since the ego is simply a collection of accumulated preferences and not a physical reality, the work becomes misdirected and therefore ineffective. Rather than patching egos to make them more internally consistent, psychotherapists would probably do better if they exposed the inappropriate strength of the preference and assisted the patient in disidentifying from it.

If someone prefers that people respect her but is sad because she is not receiving the respect of her peers at work, the person may feel this problem has caused her sadness or anger. A typical therapeutic approach would involve patching the ego. In this method, she would find ways in which her work supports her self-esteem and respect. For example, she might draw up a list of the positive results she's achieved on the job as a reminder of her merits. This might patch up her ego's belief that it must always be respected. Such a list might "prove" this point and make her feel better.

Another approach, one I believe might be more helpful, involves seeing that her belief about needing respect to be happy and healthy is flawed. If she could disidentify from the belief that her ego needs respect, her happiness would not be dependent upon others. If she sees her ego as a set of preferences (she prefers to be respected), rather than a solidified sense of self that is firm and unchanging, her sadness can lift, since her worthiness would be independent of what others say or believe. This approach offers the patient greater benefits, including the freedom to act more flexibly.

PERSONAL HURT FROM TOO SOLID AN EGO

Our ability to solidify concepts such as good/bad or heaven/hell also applies to our self-concept—who we think we are. However, all attempts at solidification distort the truth. When we solidify ourselves into one classification or another (such as Democrat/ Republican or tennis player/non-tennis player), we distort our true, flexible selves. When we solidify ourselves within a concept, threats to it can cause us psychological harm.

For example, if we come to solidify ourselves as being affiliated with a certain political party, we'll start to reject certain views simply because they're associated with another political party. Because we align ourselves with the party rather than with the merits of the situation, we lose some of the truth of the situation and may also personally come to feel less truthful. In addition, we feel injury from those of other political parties when they correctly point out our deviation from the truth. Thus, by solidifying ourselves as a member of one party, we place limits on ourselves and lose the ability to adapt and help solve specific problems as they arise.

Every time we attempt to solidify ourselves into one grouping or another, we lose some of the truth of who we are. As we add more and more solidified definitions to our self-concept, we greatly restrict our ability to be open to the changes typically required to function in modern life.

SOLIDIFICATION DUE TO THOUGHT STREAMING

Our tendency to solidify concepts doesn't stem directly from thought streaming. I believe that some biological or physiological process causes this tendency. Thought streaming may have had some evolutionary benefit, like helping us more quickly distinguish friend from foe. However, thought streaming certainly does assist the solidification process, most likely through repetition and focus.

Thought streaming often becomes involved with one particular desire (such as getting Tom to be an obedient child so he comes in from after-school play when he's called). During thought streaming episodes, we narrow our focus and examine the details of the situation from as many angles as we can. Here's how Mom can thought stream about Tom's obedience: *"Shall I try a louder voice? I wonder if I should use food as an incentive? I'll bet if I didn't let him play outside right after school that I could get him to listen to me."*

In this example this mother is excluding other, broader issues as she narrows and solidifies the concept of obedience. She may inappropriately solidify it down to one form of obedience (total obedience, immediate obedience, or happy obedience) when, in fact, obedience comes in a variety of forms. Perhaps Tom does come home, but it takes him 30 minutes to do so. Mom may want immediate obedience: *"I want you to come right home when I call you!"* But by narrowing it to immediate obedience, she may be preventing Tom from experiencing happy obedience: *"Oh, my mom always wants me home right away, but when I get home, she doesn't play with me or really want me to come right to dinner."*

As I've pointed out, thought streaming adds to the solidification of concepts. Thought streaming tends to focus our thoughts on a specific aspect of a situation, instead of on the entire picture. Thus a parent might seek total and immediate obedience in every aspect of the child's life, instead of more flexible obedience that encourages a feeling of self-worth in the child. When a real physical threat exists, such as crossing a busy intersection, a parent might demand a child's total and immediate obedience. However, when a physical threat doesn't exist, a parent might better seek cooperation from the child.

All in all, thought streaming tends to lead us away from having an open, creative mind. Instead, we're subject to the solidification of concepts. If we believe that a child's obedience must always be total and immediate, this view can cause us psychological pain and alienate the child. I believe we've all observed the potential for great harm in this.

THE PROMISE OF RELIEF

My question for psychotherapists is "From what intervention does the most effective help arise?" If the psychotherapeutic focus is on the *content* of the thoughts, we have to handle every problem that arises. We specifically need to address problems about finances, relationships, or personal capability for each situation we encounter.

Psychotherapists hope that their treatments, which try to solve one problem at a time, will generalize across life situations. With luck, patients will manage similar problems successfully in other areas of their life. However, that's just a hope. There's little data in psychotherapy on how patients generalize solutions from one situation to another. The need to prevent anxiety or any other neurotic problem from generalizing across situations remains a significant issue for psychotherapists.

However, treatment of the *process* of thought holds the promise of relief, not only for the specific and immediate problem, but also for broader situations. Such situations are content-based: We have problems with our work, home life, and personal relationships. However, thought processes are not based on specific situations; they're focused on the mental ways by which we carry and hold on to thoughts themselves. Directing our focus to the thought process promises not only the immediate relief of specific problems, but also the long-term relief of problems with a broader scope.

Free Your Mind

CHAPTER THREE

Characteristics of Thought Streaming

*"Problems cannot be solved with the same
consciousness that created them."*
—Albert Einstein

A S I mentioned in the last chapter, psychology, psychiatry, and psychotherapy failed to provide any significant relief of my anxiety and depressive symptoms. The therapies I investigated didn't spark any great insights into the origins of my troubles, their avoidance, or solution. To its credit, psychology did point the way for me to see a potentially effective therapeutic modality.

During the 1980s, I came across the title of a book with a name similar to *Thought Stopping*. That title awoke in me the sense that my *thoughts* were the problem. I, of course, did have life problems, as we all do. For each of us, life is full of them. However, that title helped me understand that while, problems are difficulties to be addressed in life, thoughts about the problems are added difficulties that only amplify the original problem.

Being interested in stopping as much mental pain in my life as possible, I decided to look into the technology used to stop thoughts. I considered that stopping thoughts was a near impossibility, but I believed that just slowing them so I could get a moment's peace would be incredibly useful. Such a moment's peace would enable me to get my bearings and rejoin the struggles in my life under improved circumstances.

Even counting sheep, that "traditional technology" that we use to get to sleep in the face of insomnia, must have been invented to help us quiet a noisy mind filled with tumultuous thoughts.

Since I've now learned that it's possible to stop thought streaming, I hope others will benefit from what I've learned. If only I could have read a book like this before my entry into psychology, it would have saved me decades of study!

THE MAIN CHARACTERISTICS OF THOUGHT STREAMS

Thought streams have three main characteristics: thought style, frequency, and the attractiveness of emotionality, or "stickiness." Perhaps there are more characteristics than these, but these appear to be the major elements. These characteristics come from looking at my own thought streaming, asking friends about theirs, and discussing thought streaming with people I've seen in therapy.

In thought streaming, one's style comes from some basic personality traits. I'll discuss these at some length in a later chapter, but for now I'll offer a brief description of the five common styles.

Thought Style

The first, a *critiquing style*, appears as a continuous mental monologue, or commentary, about quality or performance. You are engaging a critiquing style at a meal if you critique the quality of each course served in relation to good meals of the past. Example: *"The last time we were at this restaurant, the soup was good, but now it's bad. What's up with that? They had more on the menu before, but now there's much more of a limited selection."*

Next, a *checking style* operates when you mentally focus on the timelines or appropriateness of some plan. You give overly strong attention to meeting time requirements: *"I wonder if I can do the dishes in time for the good program that comes on at 8 p.m. and still have time to take the dog for a walk? I didn't see any more dishes, but I better do them now because I only have 25 minutes before that program comes on."*

In the *wandering style*, your thought streaming tends to ramble on gently from topic to topic in a less organized fashion. Here's an example: *"It's a beautiful day today, there's a nice breeze, and maybe I'll visit Rich this afternoon and see what he's up to. It will be good to go for a drive and get away from this town for a while. There are some nice stores to see on the ride to Rich's. Say, the stores in this town are getting too pricey for my taste."*

This style differs from a *wondering style* in that, while the gentle rambling seems common to both, the wondering style always includes the question "What if?" *"What if our accountant, Betty, was to leave the company for our competitor across town? We're right in the midst of expansion. What if she leaked the news to her new bosses? They could block our growth if they expanded at this critical time for us. What if they got the money but couldn't get the permit to build?"* "What if this happened? Would that be next?" is a common feature of the wondering style.

Finally, when you're engaged in the *fantasizing style*, you usually have mental monologues related to overuse of magical thinking or the outlandish. Example: *"During a full moon, I feel so warm as I am being bathed by its rays that it must be good for the Earth to receive such energy. I'm sure the plants like it, too."*

These five styles are based on common concerns or ways in which people often use their mental monologue. There may be other styles, like a planning, a catastrophizing, or a pessimistic style, but I've discovered that there are only a few overarching processes by which people organize their mental life. Have a look at your own streams of thought. Do they organize themselves in some sort of style?

Frequency of Thoughts

The next characteristic of thought streaming is thought frequency, which relates to how many thoughts per minute are occurring in the mind. Are your thoughts many or few? Is your mind racing so speedily with thoughts that your head and eyes seem to shake? Is your mind so full of thoughts that as one drops from consciousness, another comes in quickly to take its place? Alternatively, your thought frequency might be more moderate. One thought may appear in the mind, be fully considered for its value, and drop away completely, enabling some moments of thought-free space to occur before the next thought comes into consciousness.

More harm comes from rapid thought. A few thoughts at a time—for example, those supporting gentle reflection about the choice of a main dish at a restaurant—don't really bother us. At a moderate frequency, perhaps as few as five to ten thoughts arise in a minute. However, when the thought frequency increases, we become increasingly troubled. Have you ever had thoughts at the speed of thirty to sixty each minute? At such times you have no respite; your thoughts keep coming and coming and become a source of intense anxiety. In fact, you can assess your own level of anxiety by simply counting the number of thoughts you have in any given minute!

Stickiness

"Stickiness," the last quality of thought streaming, refers to the lingering quality of thought. If one particular topic of thought stays around for a long time, we say that it's "sticky." Thoughts that linger in a sticky manner typically have a stronger emotional component to them, like anger or great joy. Of course, no one minds lingering joy, but some of the stickiest thoughts are associated with anger.

For example, when we've been the object of a verbal attack, our resentment can linger on. We then can have thought streams that defend our honor, belittle the attacker, blame the circumstances, and resent those who didn't come to our defense. Here's an example: *"I didn't say that our quality control program could handle the kinds of problems that the manufacturing division is coming up with. Who the hell is Jason to put me in this kind of position? He doesn't know what my department is all about. He doesn't know all of the stress we're under here. I asked for a bigger budget, but nooo, they wouldn't give it to me. Now they want someone to blame."* The anger associated with these thoughts may cause us to have even more streaming then usual. Hours may go by as we continue to fume about the injustice.

When you know something about the style, frequency, and stickiness of thought, you grow in your ability to understand those who are troubled by a less than optimal quality of life. In contrast, when you focus exclusively on the content of one specific problematical thought or situation after another, you lack an ability to gain insight and understanding toward those who are lost in their own thought and who are troubled by its content.

I have been on both sides of the "couch," having provided psychotherapy, as well as having had therapists work with me on problems having to do with anxiety caused by a difficult personal relationship. But I obtained little relief from psychotherapy, even when it was used in combination with prescribed anti-anxiety drugs. My anxiety came from mental ruminations—loads of thoughts intruding ceaselessly in my consciousness about failure, worthlessness, broken promises, and family disappointments. My mind was firing off one negative thought after another in a seemingly endless chain as part of my interior psychological landscape.

I now know that I was actually fortunate to suffer through all that misery. It has led me to live a more compassionate life. When I provided psychotherapy services to others, I understood their pain. And I discovered that everyone suffered for the same fundamental reason: runaway thoughts about worthlessness, fear, disappointment, or failure.

The Result Is Peace

As I said in the introduction, I count as my greatest personal achievement the fact that I've stopped virtually all of my own thought streaming. Single thoughts certainly still occur, but they're now fairly well-constrained, typically limited to the initial aspect of the thought and no more. Continuous streams of thought just don't occur much within my mind anymore. I haven't suppressed them out of existence, they've just lost their fascination.

Essentially, we can't suppress individual thoughts. However, when we can understand that runaway thought streams are harmful, we can decide not to be seduced into letting them ramble on unchecked.

My present state of mind is much different from the way my mind worked just a few years ago. At that time, an initial thought would arise, change, and segue into another similar one that would again last for a while. This process would go on and on, with no real resolution to any of the thoughts.

I probably got to my current mental condition, which is happy and peaceful, because of previously having more thought streaming than I could bear. Life's problems caused me so much anxiety and mental unease that reducing that mental noise and the resulting anxiety became a focus for me. Yet a decrease in mental chatter actually increased my professional effectiveness. Recently, I have been successful as an executive in an international research company, coordinating the myriad of details involved in many projects, managing a large budget, and overseeing nearly 100 staff members, without the thought streaming many people believe is required to function effectively in this complex world. Thought streaming *is* unnecessary for good mental functioning, and if you study it carefully as I have, you will see its harmfulness much more clearly.

Mental peace and happiness, with the ability to pay attention and bring full concentration to daily activities, is available to you as well. With practice, you can stop the harmful mental chatter of thought streaming that goes on in your own mind. As I've explained, runaway thoughts are actually quite controllable. If unwanted mental noise, including songs, slogans, or longer streams of thought are keeping you from being present with your loved ones and your work, you'll certainly benefit from reading this book and practicing stopping your thought streaming.

Try This:

Find a chair, sit in a quiet place for 10 minutes, and simply watch your thoughts. At the end of 10 minutes, assess the following:

N O T I C E how many thoughts there were. Were there many or just a few? How many did you notice? Could you count them separately if you had to? Was there any break or space in the thought streaming so that a sense of quiet appeared?

S O M E T I M E S you will observe a continuous stream of thoughts in a neverending flow. With careful inspection even at these times, you can notice small separations between thoughts. This is clear consciousness free of thoughts, a very pleasant experience. Can you get a sense of it? Usually, experiencing clear consciousness encourages a desire for more of it. We often experience this in the midst of exercise or at times of concentration. But it is available to us at other times when we look behind the screen of our thought streaming.

CHAPTER FOUR

Intelligence Without Thought

"Think! How the hell are you gonna think and hit at the same time?"
—Yogi Berra

O N E aim of this book is to bring into sharper focus a few key
insights into how the mind works. The mind is a constant companion
that appears to maintain its eternal youthfulness as the body ages.
Yet much of what occurs in the mind remains either hidden from us
or dramatically obscured. I view the mind like an open space into
which thoughts and thought streams occur. Single thoughts rise up,
as the sun rises above the horizon. They remain in the mind as the
sun stays in the sky, but—and we often forget this—they set and go
away. Even without thought, the mind is still there. The mind knows
what to do and doesn't rely on thought to keep us on the right
track.

Most of us take the mental operations of our life for granted.
That is, we accept things as being a certain way, even though we
haven't looked into the facts of the matter as completely as we might.
We often mistakenly believe that thought, logical thinking, and
thought streaming control our lives. As you review the following
material, you'll see this just isn't so.

Knowing What to Do

In this book, I encourage you to look into your mental processes to gain a better understanding of them. As part of this process, we'll examine the role of logic, thought, and knowing as supports for a happy and productive life.

Animal Knowing

To begin examining some of the basics of our own mental capabilities, let's look at the intelligence of animals in nature. I'll explore a few of my favorite examples of animal behavior, which initially startled me.

As newborns, sightless marsupial pups (such as koalas) somehow wriggle their way from the birth canal up the mother's belly, nearly a foot in distance, to crawl into her pouch and locate a nipple. How do they know how to do that? Mom doesn't point the way with any hints or kind nudges. Is it a reflex action? A reflex is defined by the operation of only a few nerves and muscles, as when the physician hits the tendon below your knee with a rubber hammer to make your leg jump. Obviously, this activity in the koala is not a reflex. Yet somehow intelligence is at work, helping the pup survive.

I don't believe that thought is guiding the koala pup either. It doesn't seem reasonable to believe that the pup is thinking, *"Okay, now I need to find that pouch and nipple!"* How would it know that a pouch and a nipple even exist? Yet through the millennia, marsupial pups consistently leave the birth canal and blindly climb their way to safety and nourishment.

Many people take this activity of koala pups for granted. They assume the attitude that "It happens . . . end of story . . . a fact is a fact." However, I'd like you to reflect a bit longer on this natural event and try to figure out how it happens. I see the phenomenon as intelligence at work without thought. What's your view?

Next, monarch butterflies offer an example of another underappreciated mystery of intelligent functioning in an entirely different family of creatures. Monarchs breed four or five times a year, and every generation migrates five hundred to one thousand miles. In the summer, they flit about the southern United States, having traveled up from Mexico. In the spring, another generation leaves the Gulf coast and breeds farther north. In June, the next generation may reach Minnesota and Massachusetts.

Monarchs born in the fall somehow know not to breed, but to migrate all the way across North America to the warmer pine forests of central Mexico. They arrive there in November and remain until March of the following year, when a new generation begins the migratory cycle again. A monarch's great-great-great-great grandparents may start north from Mexico. Yet it's the great-great-great-great grandchild that somehow finds its way back to the same pine forest in Mexico that sheltered its ancestors.

Remarkable, isn't it? How do they know how to do that? As with koalas, it's hard to believe that communication goes on between monarchs (whereby, for example, the third generation tells the fourth generation how to get to Mexico). It doesn't seem likely that there are muted whispers among butterflies about taking a left turn at Tucson! The monarch migratory behavior is another example of an expression of intelligence in which thought is not involved.

You may believe that koalas and monarchs perform these completely original individual behaviors by instinct. We see similar behaviors in spiders of the same species weaving the same webs, in salmon swimming upriver to return to the place of their birth after having been in the ocean for years, in beavers lowering the water in a lake after it has frozen over and then re-blocking the dam to create a large air pocket for themselves, and in many other complex natural behaviors. But do we know any more about instinct than just that name, "instinct"? We call these behaviors "instinctual," but what is "instinct"?

Take a moment to reflect on what you or others understand about instinct. Science knows little or nothing about this fundamental process. Basically, we use the word "instinct" to indicate, by circular reasoning, that an organism completes a complex, intelligent, and specific behavior without any apparent use of the cognitive process of logic or thought. It's another way of describing intelligence without thought.

HUMAN KNOWING

When you look deeply into how we perform most of the tasks we do on a daily basis, you'll find that often, as with certain animal behaviors, we don't use logical thinking. Our minds may be ablaze with thought while we perform certain activities, but the thought is probably neither logical nor related to the activity. Rather, we typically think either about some unrelated past or present problem, or we're concerned about a problem that might arise in the future.

Let's consider an example that involves typing on a computer keyboard. See for yourself: Sit at a keyboard and give it a try. What happens mentally when we're involved in the complex process of typing? Are we engaged in logical thinking as our fingers move from key to key? No. Are we having general thoughts about our next meal or our personal relationships? No. Our mind is simply open and alert. We're typing on the keys and being generally attentive to the text we're trying to enter.

What happens when we're moving right along with the correct keystrokes and some thoughts come into our mind? We might think,

"I feel sad that Katie has the flu. I wonder where she got it. I hope it wasn't from her boyfriend Al. That would make them both sick at the same time." In thinking about our child's flu or worrying about carpal tunnel syndrome, we actually have to stop typing because our work will begin to have errors. We can return to typing only when all that mental noise subsides. Thus we don't use our thinking processes as we type. However, it's equally incorrect to say that we type by instinct.

Consider whether you use thought or logical thinking to drive your car. My own experience shows that we learn to drive and then "know" how to do so. Driving doesn't require any formal use of logic. Nor does our internal monologue assist us in carrying out this action. We don't use a mental monologue such as, *"I see a stop sign up ahead. I must apply the brake at a moderate level so I'll come to a quick, smooth stop 15 feet behind that blue car up ahead."* Actually, we often drive while having a variety of thoughts completely unrelated to the driving, yet we drive in spite of them. Thus, as with typing, we can drive our car efficiently and skillfully without logic and cognitive thought.

Finally, when we're asleep at night and find ourselves too cold, what do we do? Without engaging our thinking mind, we pull on more covers. We even sense that we should not engage our thinking mind as we pull up the covers because we risk becoming involved in thinking that would prevent us from going quickly back to sleep. Again, we can and do act intelligently without logical thinking. We usually believe we carry out most of our daily activities primarily using our thoughts for direction, but we're quite wrong.

THE NEED TO CURTAIL THE THINKING PROCESS
According to baseball and literary giant Yogi Berra, *"Think! How*

the hell are you gonna think and hit at the same time?" This quotation shows that the need to curtail the thinking process also relates to successfully playing baseball. A batter simply can't think and hit at the same time. Certainly between pitches he may have thoughts, such as *"I wonder where he'll throw next? High and inside, I bet! It was only last month that he hit me, too. I hope it doesn't happen again. I also have to deal with this ump who calls a high strike zone."* However, these thoughts actually impair the batter's ability to hit. When baseball players hit, catch, throw the ball, and take part in all other active aspects of the game, *no thinking is involved.* How, then, do we know whether to swing high or low to hit the ball? We just know what to do. And we find the process to be remarkably dependable!

We all engage in many activities in which we don't use either thought or formal logic, but we still get the job done completely. In fact, often we *must not* use logic or thinking to best perform an activity. Here are a number of widely different examples:

- We can't read and think at the same time. We actually need to block any extraneous thinking to concentrate on the words in front of us.
- Golf coaches encourage us to stop and calm our minds, emptying them of thoughts so we can focus on the crucial task of putting.
- We can't give a speech to an audience if our mind is filled with thoughts.
- We can play better chess with a mind that's able to concentrate than with a mind full of many different thoughts.
- We can speak to someone more intimately, and we can better understand what he or she is saying if our thoughts are quiet.
- When we're shopping, we can't examine an item's quality or workmanship well if distracting thoughts are bothering us.

If we reflect on our personal experience, we see that we actually complete many of our activities *in spite of* our thoughts! Yet most people mistakenly believe that the guiding principle ruling the day-to-day practicalities of life is thinking. The examples I've just presented clearly show that, quite the contrary, *stopping* the occurrence of thought is required for many activities. This is amazing when you truly consider it! We perform most of our activities best without logical thinking and distracting streams of thought. I believe that on any given day, we act by "knowing" 98 percent of the time, we act by logic 1 percent of the time, and utilize insight the remaining 1 percent. Unfortunately, because we don't trust our "knowing," we unnecessarily thought stream 98 percent of the day too. Please take a moment to digest this information, which shatters basic views about how we carry out our lives. Considering even these few examples, you can see how most of us greatly overestimate the need for thought.

LOVING OUR BEINGNESS

At this point we should begin to wonder about the value of thought and its proliferating nature. We take thought streaming for granted because it seems a necessary and fundamental aspect of being human. But not only should we question the value of thought, we should also examine its detrimental effects.

As I've indicated, thought streams impair our ability to pay attention and prevent us from living lives that are more intimate. Yet most of us haven't considered the full impact of thought streaming on our lives. So far we've considered many ways in which we act without engaging in mental monologue, and we've seen that thought streaming is superfluous, an additional but not required way we can use our mind. All of us would like to have a clear mind, one unclouded by thought streaming, but we just don't fully appreciate how much. For instance, I believe that all recreation is unknowingly aimed at reducing thought streaming. We so much love the fundamental "beingness" that exists behind our screen of thoughts that we're willing to skydive, crochet, bungee jump, run distances, play golf or tennis, and engage in a wide variety of less strenuous activities to experience the sense of aliveness unclouded by thought. We fail to see that the feeling these sports and activities provide— our sense of beingness—is available to us at other times simply when our thought streaming subsides.

For people with wildly uncontrolled thought streaming, it may take extreme sports to sufficiently block their thoughts so they can feel the basic aliveness of their being. For others with less problematic thought streaming, milder forms of exercise or activities requiring focused concentration may allow the return to that joyful sense of aliveness at the heart of being.

Clearly, rampant thought streaming blocks and obscures our felt sense of aliveness. If we lose this sense, we truly lose most of life's value; that's why many of us will go to great extremes of activity to regain it. We really do miss it when thought streaming obscures it.

TRY THIS:

Find a chair, sit in a quiet place for 10 minutes, and simply watch your thoughts. At the end of each minute, take a moment to assess the following.

N O W that you can notice your thoughts, after each minute of observing, ask yourself, *"How important did each thought seem? Was each thought helpful in your life?"* How many of your thoughts were required for you to function? Be truthful! How many were about "worry" or "concern" however strong or mild?

W E R E your worried or concerned thoughts truly helpful to you? Consider whether you need to worry about an upcoming problem or whether you feel you can actually deal with it later when the time comes. You needn't answer this question now, but these are good questions to keep under consideration.

FREE YOUR MIND

CHAPTER FIVE

Our Mental Processes: Logical Thinking and Insight

*"With perfect attention, habitual abstract
mental structures melt away."*
—Steven Pashko, Ph.D.

A S I wrote in a previous chapter, looking for meaning in words or symbols is often like looking at the fossilized remains of one of our early human ancestors. We examine the fossil content from a variety of angles: carbon dating, structural comparison to other primates and hominids, microscopic comparison to other fossilized remains, and so on. Yet when we complete the examinations, we don't get a true sense of the most meaningful aspect of their life: how happy our human ancestors really were!

We can say the same thing about the content of our own thoughts. We may consider certain aspects in great detail. Through this "analysis" of sorts, we believe we've understood much about the situation (such as others' hidden motivations or why he and she don't get along). Too often, however, we're just dancing in our head—mistaking a true compliment for sarcasm, overrating our importance to others as we worry about clothing coordination, and believing an expensive car can enhance our own personal value.

With symbolic meaning, for instance, who can say for certain that a boat in a dream means anything at all? Perhaps you saw a boat earlier in the day. Perhaps you remembered your father and the good times you had with him on his boat. Somehow our world is filled with this kind of analysis; we vigorously try to figure out deep meaning when, in fact, reality may be self-evident. At times, we pursue details to an amazing extent. When an important live discussion is held in Congress, for example, news commentators analyze it right after it finishes. Other experts review the event on the evening news, pundits comment on it on the weekends and write editorials in the Sunday paper. Do we need these multiple re-analyses? Did we learn anything new? I think not. We can stop watching this kind of activity on television, and in the same way, we can stop doing this activity in our head. If we made this simple but significant change, our lives would certainly improve.

PROCESS VS. CONTENT

Because we trivialize the *process* of mental events in favor of an undue focus on their *content*, psychotherapy suffers in effectiveness. Even if we're not in therapy, we all look too much to the content of our thoughts in trying to extract subtle shades of meaning. We analyze the words others say to us ("You look nice today.") to find the hidden meanings (*"I wonder if she's being sarcastic, because I'm sure my belt isn't the same color as my shoes."*) We worry about symbols, for example, like the social status conferred upon us by our car. We take our own negative emotions as indicators of personal failure. We believe that thoughts about food mean we're hungry and that a dream about a boat means we need a vacation on a tropical isle. Marketers tap into this proclivity of ours by encouraging us to buy their vacation packages or luxury products.

Thoughts universally occur without our wanting them. Many

occur repetitively. They probably result from the spontaneous activity of tonic neurons, brain cells that fire regularly or periodically like the pacemaker cells of our heart. If we want to better understand our own mental condition, we must look more closely at the process of thought streaming itself. Examining both the process as well as the content of thought will give us a more complete understanding of our own mental condition than would our usual reliance on content alone.

The Mental Monologue

We can best understand the cognitive mental activity involved in thought by dividing it into three aspects: logical thinking, single-thought occurrence, and thought streaming. Let's look at each in turn.

Logical Thinking

I define logical thinking as the action of using one's mind to produce thoughts. For example, when we go through the forms and instructions in doing our taxes, we enter the true process of logical thinking. The inner monologue may go something like this: *"This form starts with gross income. Here's the first deduction. I can take some percentage of this amount. Seven plus three, one plus six plus two, eight plus nine . . ."*

This example shows a few of the characteristics of logical thinking. First, it's a voluntary process. Each of us *initiates* logical thinking. For example, we choose to think logically about the menu we'll create for our next meal or the requirements of building a bridge over a roadway. Second, it's a directed process that follows a straightforward path to solve a specific problem. Third, it uses some type of formal logic system, such as arithmetic, date and time planning, or priority ordering. In our tax example, we used the formal logic system of arithmetic to sum up deductions applied to our gross income. This useful and practical process has many benefits.

Logical thinking most often occurs when we're solving an immediate problem. Vague planning about a vacation to a faraway island tends not to be logical thinking if we're thought streaming about securing travel connections or worrying about other ways our plans may go awry. Logical thinking takes place when we're finalizing our plans by making specific flight arrangements and hotel and rental car reservations. Example: *"If we change planes in Salt Lake City, we can stay there for a few days and ski without any extra costs."*

Finally, thinking often has a mental noise associated with it. The tax example shows that we silently say the numbers internally to ourselves as we follow the logical steps needed to complete our forms.

Let me now ask you a fundamental question about your use of the word "thinking." We often use the word in day-to-day speech, but many of us haven't taken a good look at the actual thinking process. When someone asks you to think about an issue and offer an opinion, how would you describe your thinking process? When I consider how I think, I don't often use true logic. I don't carefully weigh the pros and cons, using a formal logic system to come up with an answer. I usually assess my preferences and state my opinion based on them.

I believe that most people don't use a formal, rule-based, logical thinking process when asked to "think" about something. We tend to consider a problem and come up with an answer based on a thinking-free judgment. Apart from making specific plans, doing arithmetic problems, and calculating our taxes, we don't really use true logical thinking during much of life.

For example, I have bought and sold a few houses during my many, mostly job-related moves. I bought a house in Virginia, and I did think about location, size, number of bedrooms, commute time, and many other factors. My thought process went like this: "*I need to get a den or office so I have a place to work from when I'm at home. That's really important.*" However, when I actually made the decision, the nice backyard deck overruled many important factors. It was large, had nice trees around it, and I could relax in privacy. Did I use logic to make this decision? Not really. The house (actually a townhouse) was smaller than I wanted, had only two bedrooms, and didn't have a den or office. Did I think about the house? Yes, I did. But I really only entertained thought streaming about it. While I reflected on the benefits of the house, I didn't make the purchase logically. I generally buy cars this same way. Logic says one thing, and some vague preference in me says another. Usually, I act on that vague sense of preference.

My definition of logical thinking—the action of using one's mind to produce thoughts—points to a significant problem with the word "thinking". The definition indicates that thinking is a directed, rational, and voluntary process, one in which an action occurs and the mind produces logical thoughts to accomplish an immediate task. However, haven't we all been in countless situations when we weren't voluntarily using the mind to produce thoughts, yet they kept coming anyway? The thoughts that pester us at bedtime, right when we want to fall asleep, serve as a perfect example of such unwanted thoughts.

Therefore, we need to expand our definition of thought to include passive, involuntary, and unwanted mental discourse. I've looked in a variety of dictionaries yet can't find a definition for passive thinking. So, I suggest we use the word "thoughting."

Thoughting

Let's define thoughting as "the act or process of a *single* thought coming into consciousness when it is not intentionally desired."

We can see how specific word usage is needed, since logical thinking is clearly different from what we're now calling "thoughting." We've all experienced both these mental processes, but we haven't taken the time to distinguish between the two.

Although logical thinking is an active and voluntary process, thoughting (also known as "having a single thought or a flash of thought") is not. It is passive and involuntary. While a burst of logical thinking may last for a few minutes, instances of thoughting are, by definition, extremely short-lived.

Individual thoughts arrive at any time and last only a moment, perhaps less than a second in duration. A thought about food may pop into consciousness when we haven't eaten for a while. A critical thought about someone's driving may come up on the highway. Thoughts about tasting something sweet, remembering a good time we had, or planning to get a tune-up on the car exemplify the quick, passive, and involuntary process of thoughting. Other examples include, "*Oh, I need gas. Time for lunch. Ah, Jerry likes Superman stories. E does equal MC squared. Sally likes me.*"

Insights represent a specific type of this kind of thought. We all have insights, which are brief openings into fundamental intelligence—the origin of how we know things. Typically, they are our "good ideas." We don't logically "think up" good ideas; they actually come to us. And once an insight occurs, it can continue to be quite useful because the knowledge it provides stays with us. We can use an insight's wisdom for many years, generalizing it across a wide variety of experiences.

Let's take a moment to consider insights, which can be grand or small. Einstein's insight on the theory of relativity was grand. When we're children, our first understanding of how multiplication represents serial addition comes through a smaller but no less significant insight. Our arithmetic teachers coach us toward having this insight, but ultimately we have to see the relationship for ourselves.

In American English, we have an expression about a thought "dawning" on us. This expression describes the impact and manner of delivery of an insight. We don't know how it occurs, so we say metaphorically that it "dawns" on us, which indicates the experience of sudden, involuntary, and enhanced access to a deeper form of knowing. The last time a good idea dawned on you, you probably remember that it didn't come through logical thought. Can you remember the "aha" experience you felt?

As an example, when we "get" the insight that a map is a symbolic representation of geography, we can use this understanding throughout our entire lifetime. We receive this insight in a flash of knowledge and then apply it each time we use a different type of map. We then can extend our range of "maps" to include reading blueprints, deciphering diagrams on how to attach stereo speakers, and figuring out how to arrange pieces of fabric to make a complete shirt. We also become so comfortable with maps that we don't worry about finding a distant travel destination, even though we haven't driven there before.

Solutions to particularly troubling crossword puzzles come from insights into how the puzzle's author has made unique connections between two ideas or concepts. We can use memory recall to answer the easier questions, but for the more difficult ones we must rely on insight. For example, we need an insight to come up with a six-letter word for "the sound of getting by." After we hear the answer, we typically say, "Oh, yeah!" indicating that an insight has occurred. I sometimes wonder whether people who like to do crossword puzzles especially enjoy opening their minds to insights. I also wonder whether we can train our mind to have more insights just by doing crossword puzzles! (By the way, the answer is "squeak.")

Varieties of Insights

In the following brief list, I look at some varieties of insights that we all have in day-to-day life. They may seem fundamental and matter-of-fact, but essentially they come to us not through rote learning, but through knowledge that dawns on us through insight.

The Representational Insight

When we have a representational insight, we understand that words point to objects and conditions. We realize that sounds can represent objects; for example, the word "tree" points to a woody perennial plant with a trunk and many branches. Similarly, roadmaps show the path of a route, and we can use numbers to express amounts.

I was once privileged to witness an infant first associating herself with her name. The baby's name was Sarah, and her mother had brought her along to the clinic in which I worked. I was stopping by to see this cute little girl when I heard her mother saying her name.

Sarah's mom would point to her and say "Sar-ah," then turn her finger around and say "Mom-my." Back and forth it went: "Sarah, Mom-my, Sar-ah." One of the times that her mother said "Sar-ah," the baby's eyes widened and her whole face lit up. We could tell that she had just made the first connection between herself and the name representing her. All of us in the waiting room laughed with delight.

The Arithmetical Insight

When you have an arithmetical insight, you realize that addition and subtraction are related to multiplication and division, that the number zero exists and is endlessly useful, and so forth.

I remember my own "aha" experience when I first understood the relationship between multiplication and addition. I was at home, grudgingly practicing my "times tables." My parents wanted me to learn them, and when I had memorized each evening's required quota, I would demonstrate this aloud for them.

What a feeling when it suddenly became clear to me that 7 + 7 + 7 was the same as 7 x 3! It may have been an "aha" of minor magnitude in the big scheme of things, but I won't forget the experience. Nor will I forget the overall relationship between addition and multiplication. From that time on, I've made use of that particular insight innumerable times. One momentary flash of insight into knowledge provides a lifetime of new capability.

The Mechanical Insight

A mechanical insight lets you see how work is made easier through using devices, such as screws, wedges, levers, pulleys, wheels and axles, and inclined planes.

I spent some happy hours of my childhood helping my father in construction. As a structural ironworker, he helped put up the steel frames of large buildings. The columns and beams typically went up by crane, since they were too heavy to lift. Assisted by the crane, two men would put a beam in place and tighten it down with only one or two bolts. Others would come by later to fill in additional bolts—typically five to ten more—and make sure the beam was appropriately secured. I became one of these workers.

I saw that getting the holes of one beam to match up with the holes in one or two others was a challenge. Beams can weigh a few tons, and the clearances needed to line up their twenty holes are often very tight. A moment of mechanical insight dawned on me when my father showed me the use of high-strength, eight-inch, tapered steel pins. The wedging action of these three-pound pins, when combined with solid blows from a sledgehammer, made tons of steel move around exactly as needed. So that was how people could manage to move big beams to within tight tolerances! At that moment, I further realized that such slim wedges could also be placed under steel columns so that entire walls could be made plumb.

The Interpersonal Insight

An interpersonal insight lets me know that you and I are alike. I realize that, while certain things hurt me, and others bring me joy, you, too, feel the same hurts and joys. Consequently, if I want to understand your feelings, interests, or motivations, I can look to mine, since we're similar in this way, no matter how our cultures or backgrounds may differ.

I've watched small children between the ages of three and four playing together in beach sand with plastic pails and shovels. They might make sand castles, create abstract designs, or just have fun digging holes. When a child gets upset, she may strike another child with one of her toys. Something wonderful happens when the playmate hits back: You can see the surprise on the original antagonist's face. She has found herself being hurt in a cause-and-effect way.

Clearly, such children are learning not to hit others. At the same time, they're having an interpersonal insight about empathy and compassion. They're realizing that the retaliatory hurt they've received is the same hurt felt by their friend.

The Fire Insight

This especially primal insight occurs when you realize that fire can be made in a number of different ways, that it can be used as a kind of servant (for warmth or cooking, for example), but that it also can be a powerful source of danger.

I don't remember having any personal insights about fire, although I'm sure I've had my share. Perhaps you can remember some of your own. However, I do think about our human ancestors and how they must have experienced their initial insights about fire. Can't you just picture the glee on their faces as they realized the uses of fire?

While many of the insights I've discussed are grand in scope and importance, probably all of them date back to prehistoric times. Many of them were certainly species-changing events.

Each of us has to use these insights to function as ordinary humans. Can you imagine a person today who doesn't know about maps, words, tools, or fire? In fact, to prepare us for these insights, societies set up educational systems so that we can each have these insights and then learn techniques for using them. Countless other insights exist; I've simply identified a few examples. Feel free to remind yourself of others that have happened in your own life. Despite being modest or appearing relatively unnoticed in their initial phases, insights always have a significance that carries on way past their initial occurrence.

It's my assertion and a core assumption of this book that insight is the only way we can solve difficult problems. We mistakenly believe that solutions come to us through logical thinking. While this is true to some extent, it's not the complete truth. I find it useful to distinguish between insight and knowing on the one hand, and learning and understanding on the other. Although we have blurred the definitional lines, if we don't make a clear distinction between the two pairs, we neglect the importance of the only process that has the true capability of helping us solve our most difficult problems.

Time and again, we have tried logical approaches to solving the greatest of our human problems, such as global famine; limited access to affordable health care and housing; and prejudice, whether personal, gender, religious, tribal, racial, or national. Our logical approaches suffer from serious shortcomings, since they simply rearrange surface situations in a variety of logical ways without using insight to plumb the depths of these problems and provide effective solutions.

As a logical response to famine in Africa, many people have raised money to feed the starving and truly needy. Yet just a short while later, the food runs out and the famine returns. Most people understand that the land is too unproductive and that there are too many mouths to feed, but they lack of insight in dealing with local beliefs about property ownership, tribal prejudice, and nationalism thwarting any hopes for a long-term solution. In the Middle East, people kill enemies, build walls, and exclude certain groups from participating in community solutions to problems. They do this through logical arguments based on concepts of sovereignty, self-rule, self-determination, and morality. They rarely use insight to transcend religious divisiveness and to share their commonality. Nor do they use insight to foster a sense of regional community for the benefit of the many.

Unfortunately, how we come to an insight remains a mystery. I recommend that, as a culture, we take up the analysis of insight as a field of study. I also believe that we should personally look into this phenomenon within ourselves. Insights come to us as a great blessing, and studying them offers us great potential benefit.

However, I find little in the scientific literature about how to have an insight. No training manual or readily available book offers tips for efficiently cultivating insights. If you have further interest in cultivating insights, I suggest you do more reading in the areas of art, creativity, and meditation. From my own experience of formal academic study, additional reading, and years of meditation, I see that insight comes more readily when my mind isn't obscured by thought streaming and previously formed opinions or beliefs. You can prepare for an insight through logic, reason, and information that you gather about an issue. Yet if you cultivate open awareness and have a mind unclouded by thought streaming, insights more readily appear. If you can decrease thought streaming and hold prejudgment at bay, you'll increase your likelihood of receiving insights.

FREE YOUR MIND

CHAPTER SIX

An In-depth Look at Thought Streaming

"All your thought streaming is harmful."
—Steven Pashko, Ph.D.

I ' V E formed the word "thought streaming" through a new combination of words. I define it as "the process whereby one thought occurs and other associated or tangential thoughts follow in relatively rapid order."

Take the example of a man who is trying to fall asleep but who is being kept awake by thought. We can clearly follow the flow of his thought streaming: *"I wonder if Karla is pregnant. I hope she is. I wonder if she knows and isn't telling me. I hope she's happy about it. She doesn't look happy."* This person isn't actively seeking thoughts; they're involuntarily coming into his mind. Unwanted thought follows unwanted thought, each with its own brand of quasi-logic, but they lack direction to help solve a problem. Sometimes we compulsively reenact a scenario that occurred earlier in the day or week. Yet replaying the scenario won't help solve a problem, but will actually cause another—sleeplessness!

To show that thought streaming doesn't just occur at night when we're ready to sleep, let's look at other examples. We notice thought streaming at night because that's the time we need mental quiet.

However, have you ever tried to read a book or magazine and had thought streaming break your concentration? All of us have had this happen. At these times, we're truly lost in thought. Instead of letting you read, your thought streams drag your mental focus off into remembering mean bosses, delicious meals, or complicated personal relationships you've had.

Have you ever sat in a bus station, train station, or airport and watched people walk by? What would have been your typical mental activity at such a time? Was it active, voluntary, and logical thinking or thought streaming? I'll put my bet on thought streaming because that's how the mind often acts when it's not engaged in any specific task requiring its attention. Here's an example: *"Wow, is that person in a hurry! She walks kind of weird, with her arms out to the side too much. Talk about luggage: How much can this guy carry? He could be away for years with all that stuff!"*

Thought streaming appears in many forms. You can most easily identify it when you need to concentrate or pay attention because that's when you can see its concentration-blocking effects. At such times, it shows up more clearly as being involuntary and unwanted. When you're waiting in a train station, with no need to focus your attention on anything specific, thought streaming seems more difficult to distinguish from thinking. But if you'll take a close look at your mental activity in such a situation, you'll notice that whenever mental quiet is potentially available, thought streaming tends to jump in—either to provide relief from boredom or to disrupt any true mental peace.

Please note there may or may not be a central theme, such as hunger or a personal relationship, to any of your thought streaming. Essentially, unsolicited thoughts just keep coming and coming.

As I've mentioned before, the most serious manifestation of

thought streaming is the mental disease known as obsessive-compulsive disorder. Jack Nicholson gave a good portrayal of a man afflicted with this disorder in the film As Good As It Gets. Most of us, though, must concern ourselves with only the less bothersome (though still serious) problem of thought streaming.

When thought streaming occurs, the mind skips along from topic to topic, often in an elaborate, unceasing internal monologue. Some call it our "stream of consciousness"; others refer to it as "daydreaming," "mental chatter," or "being lost in thought." When thoughts have little emotional content, thought streaming can feel light and breezy, like thoughts of a warm and inviting beach. But when thoughts have a high emotional content, thought streaming can feel quite heavy, as when we have thoughts of anger or worthlessness.

Thought streaming differs from thinking in that it has much less focus. Thinking is an orderly process. You can make vacation reservations, write down a grocery list, or design something as complex as a bridge using logical thinking. In contrast, thought streaming is more like mental rambling, often characterized by a sense of randomness. At times I've heard people say, "I wonder why all these thoughts are linked together." In my own experience, I've noticed my thoughts jumping in rapid order from one subject to another vaguely related subject.

Because thought streaming isn't linked to any insight, it can't assist us in problem solving. At best, thought streaming can only dredge up seemingly related ideas and juxtapose them so we can see both concepts at once. However, the combination that results is typically more a mixture of odd mental elements rather than a helpful relationship between two concepts.

Why We Thought Stream

There are three reasons why we thought stream. First, we make a basic error in assuming that because thought streams seem similar to logical thinking (in that both use an internal mental monologue), we can use thought streams to find answers to problems. Basically, we don't trust our inner knowing, our fundamental intelligence, to solve our problems. Yet when thought streaming is absent, intelligence knows how to putt a ball, compose a song, and crochet a scarf. Spiders of the same species build identical, complex webs; butterflies migrate; and koala pups find pouches using this same intelligence.

Lacking confidence in his inner knowing, Paul, the human resources recruiter mentioned earlier in the book, mistakenly encouraged thought streaming to help him deal with prostate cancer. Although he was waiting for the results of his biopsy, he encouraged his thought streams to find possible ways to relieve the grief his wife might feel and to get his daughter through art school. But these problems and his cancer did not yet exist. Remember, he only had a biopsy, and there was no diagnosis of cancer. Was he really solving any problem? Obviously, he was not. When we mistakenly believe that thought streaming helps solve problems, we either actively encourage them or passively allow them to keep going because we believe they are helpful. When we hold this belief, we fall prey to the *primary error of thought streaming*, which I'll describe in more detail a little later in this book.

The second reason why we thought stream involves our search for emotional security. We like to feel as if we're in control, even when logically we know we aren't. In an attempt to retain a sense of emotional control, we use every possible resource we have, even if it's weak and ineffectual. In the vague belief that thought streaming may help us find a solution to our problems, we encourage it. We believe that it adds to our vigilance against threats of failure; that it might help us solve a problem; or that we're taking some form of positive action when we really don't know what else to do. In reality, it doesn't add to our vigilance, doesn't help us solve problems, and isn't a positive action. Thought streaming only drains us mentally and causes worry. I doubt that we would allow thought streams to persist if we truly knew their cost to our lives.

Ironically, we need to overcome the fear of being out of control based on the mistaken belief that our thought streams help us solve problems to gain control of our mental thought-streaming processes. We need to realize that thought streaming itself causes problems and blocks the mental clarity required for the best problem solving. Once we overcome our fear of being out of control by having this insight, we find more security in our primordial intelligence and trust it more than we do any stream of thoughts we ever had.

The final reason why we thought stream is that we are encouraged to do so by our society. Marketing is a basic aspect of business, which drives much of America. Marketers seek to convince us that their products are worth buying. In doing so, they often create a sense of lack or incompleteness within us. They then position their products as the items or services to fill these artificially created needs. Commercial messages typically promise that our self-esteem will increase and we'll be "normal" if we buy a certain car or a piece of jewelry. Marketers encourage us to buy what we don't have and do what we aren't doing enough of, such as taking lavish vacations and getting our "quota" of fun. These messages encourage thought streaming. They make us fantasize about how our life would be different if we purchased a luxury car, vacationed on an exotic island in the South Seas, or enhanced our appearance through cosmetic surgery. Before knowing about the harmful effects of thought streaming, we aren't so concerned about advertisers' subtle, hidden influence in our life. However, once we wake up to the dangers of thought streaming, we'll be more skeptical about the claims that marketers make in their commercial messages.

HOW IT GETS STARTED

Thought streaming usually begins innocently enough, and it often goes quite unnoticed. Once it starts (and for many of us it seldom ceases except as we fall off to sleep), it typically accelerates out of control.

As an example, let's examine how a thought streaming sequence begins, triggered by an initial feeling of hunger and leading to the first thought about our next meal.

After this first thought has occurred, another thought takes us on a mental tangent. Let's say the first thought changes into one about what food we'd prefer to eat (*"I'm in the mood for a big club sandwich."*) This thought may then stir a worry about eating too much of our favorite foods (*"I wonder if eating these sandwiches every day is healthy."*)

Then, because we've had the thought about eating too much of certain foods, a thought about being overweight might enter into this thought stream (*"I'm kind of packing on the pounds lately; I wonder if it's the sandwiches."*)

At this point, the thoughts just keep coming, one after another. Perhaps they're self-critical thoughts about being overweight (*"Man, I'm starting to look like this sandwich."*) Perhaps they're guilty thoughts about how not looking our best influences our career and social life (*"I'm losing job opportunities because I can't control my eating."*)

Thought streams can and do go on if we don't control them. In some people, the stream is fairly continuous; in others, it stops and goes (but often with more going than stopping).

Self-Generated "Entertainment"

Most of us don't know that, either directly or indirectly, we encourage our own thought streams. Is this hard to accept? You might not think that you're doing anything to encourage those last bothersome thoughts before you go to sleep. You might be right, too—but only for that specific time of the day. Somehow, we all have the capability to discourage thought streams. How else could we shut off our minds at bedtime and fall asleep? So, yes, we can control them. But mostly we don't practice controlling them. In fact, often we do just the opposite: We encourage them, especially when we're bored and want some entertainment.

Our own thoughts provide us with the cheapest entertainment available. You can confirm this in your own experience. When you want to distract yourself for any given reason, you can voluntarily summon thought streams, look at various issues from all sides, and see how they relate to other thought streams you call forth. You can run one scenario after another in rapid order, for minutes or hours on end. Some people spend their lives doing nothing but this! Their thought streams act like the commentary on the commentary about a news story. It can be very entertaining—that is, until you want to shut off this process of relentless thought. Having practiced initiating and maintaining thoughts for so long, we all find it difficult, if not seemingly impossible, to shut them off.

Clearly we have bothersome and even destructive thought streams because we haven't practiced the discipline of ceasing interest in or breaking free of them at will. As we begin to have a quieter mind, we experience great mental relief and an ability to better carry out our numerous activities. Imagine walking through the world and directly experiencing its wonders without a screen of sad, guilty, anxious, criticizing, fantasizing, or even pleasant thoughts interfering with your experience.

Missing from your life (but not missed) would be the internal monologue that continuously comments on all circumstances, reflects on all activities, and provides detailed plans of what should occur next in your life. Gone would also be all those worried, anxious thoughts about dealing with situations you can't control.

Wouldn't it be great to escape all that unsatisfactory, useless mental noise? Can you imagine a life with no worrisome thoughts? Would you like a life characterized by an ability to pay attention, with no screen of interfering thoughts? Can you imagine putting a golf ball without distraction, reading with full concentration, attending fully to your customer during a sales call, speaking without second-guessing yourself, and deeply feeling the intimacy that another has to offer? To live this fully, you need to develop the continuous attention required for stopping each thought from going quickly on to the next ones. Each effort will result in a small gain, and consistent effort over a longer time will yield incredible results, including a profound felt sense of mental relief.

THE PRIMARY ERROR ABOUT LOGICAL THINKING

Most people make a significant error about the use and purpose of logical thinking. As I described previously, many of us incorrectly believe that we get answers to our fundamental questions by thinking about them. When we make this *primary error about logical thinking*, believing that it solves significant problems, we unknowingly ensure that they continue unsolved, as evidenced by the intractable conflicts we face in the world today.

I reiterate, however, that the answers to our most fundamental and troubling problems and questions come exclusively from the insights that occur more frequently than we realize. As I've said, insights show up through a completely different process than logical thinking or the thought-streaming process. Whereas the results of logical thinking may help us cope better with daily issues, insights have substantially beneficial effects on our life for decades. Because insights are so useful and powerful, we could benefit significantly by having many more of them. Too often, though, we settle for answers derived from logical thinking when we really need solutions of more depth and wisdom, like those provided by insights.

I don't need to remind you that humankind has many problems. To solve them, numerous solutions have been tried. Yet we still have long-standing problems whose solutions elude us. To resolve these more difficult problems that face us all, we need insights. Logical thinking just doesn't have the power.

The following is a short list of the fundamental and intractable problems we face:

1. We adamantly hold on to our judgments about what is right and wrong rather than extending compassion to other beings. For example, the belief that alcoholism stems from a weak sense of morality may prevent someone from extending a helping hand to a street person in obvious physical distress.

2. We insist on maintaining religious stances of right and wrong rather than extending our compassion to other beings. For example, a religious belief that supports the idea of male superiority may prevent someone from assisting a woman who is married to an abusive spouse.

3. We adhere to political stances of right and wrong rather

than extending our compassion to other beings. For instance, the political status of a certain nation may prevent its citizens from receiving food or medical aid.

4. We separate ourselves from others in our thinking and attitude, which creates conflict. For instance, a divisive-minded person may seek to gain wealth, power, or love at the expense of others.

5. We're stuck in our concepts, whose arbitrary distinctions and categorizations cause conflict. For instance, all people may have genetically originated as Africans, yet we use racial categorizations as distinctions, not as commonalities.

Although this short list is broad and general, it encompasses many of the personal, racial, ethnic, national, religious, and gender problems we face. There are only a few fundamental causes of human conflict, yet they persist as problems because we've tried to solve them through the more or less exclusive use of logical thinking.

In the examples above, we see the origins of past and current wars, as well as the potential for future conflicts. The basis for the "have" versus "have not" mentality that seeks to separate one artificially conceptualized group from another exists in these examples, as does the artificially created basis of superior and inferior roles.

To overcome such problems as famine, racism, genocide, pollution, and religious intolerance, we need insight into them. We don't have it yet globally, and that's what's making these problems insoluble. We're trying to apply logical thinking to problems that actually require new insights.

In trying to solve age-old problems like religious intolerance, we think more communication will help, so we set up conferences. We figure that study of the "other" religion may help, so we read their texts. We suppose that personalizing the problem may help, so we live among people with different religious beliefs. We think up many potential solutions, yet none really work—perhaps because while we're thinking up possible solutions, we're consistently retaining our own beliefs.

Our beliefs aren't based on thinking, but on an internal sensibility that's formed outside the world of logic. We don't change our beliefs based on thinking—only on insight. We may believe that children need to be protected from physical threats, like falling off swings, being stung by bees, getting diseases from other children at nursery school, and hitting their heads on the corners of kitchen countertops. Logic dictates they shouldn't use swings, play outside, or go to nursery school, and we put rubber bumpers along our countertops. The insight that overprotection may itself cause harm to our children needs to occur before we can change our belief that "safer is always better." Only when we have insights about the counterproductive beliefs we hold can we remove their underpinnings and see better times prevail.

The Primary Error About Thought Streaming

As I just mentioned, we incorrectly associate logical thinking as the way we get answers to all our problems. In so doing, we also incorrectly look to another apparently similar process. In attempting to solve our problems, we often turn to thought streaming because of its apparent but invalid similarity with logical thinking. We confuse the two processes because both involve an internal monologue. Also, both appear to help us make conceptual links between and among concepts.

However, while these processes appear to be similar activities, they're actually quite different. Logical thinking holds a certain validity because it concerns reaching an understanding through logical processes and solutions. Thought streaming, however, has no such a connection to a logical system. Rather, it makes only obsessive associations between and among ideas and concepts.

Because of the primary error about thought streaming, we believe that logical thinking and thought streaming are either similar or identical. While thought streaming has no ability to solve problems using logic, we mistakenly believe it does. This error makes it responsible for much of the pain and suffering that people experience. It's also the main motivating factor that keeps us interested in our own harmful thought streaming. The sooner we realize this, the sooner we'll ease our troubles.

The inappropriate use of thought streaming often begins when we remember a past experience, perhaps about being late to meeting a friend because the car wouldn't start. As we direct our mental monologue toward the problem, we mentally review a few scenarios about possible solutions: *"Darn this car! I always buy bad cars! Sometimes my cars wouldn't start because my battery was old and weak. That was my really old car. It was a good car when it was new, but it got old and ugly and fell apart quickly. Sometimes my starter went bad, and one time I just ran out of gas."* Eventually, we use logic to identify the one solution that best fits the specific problem. Finally, we take action using that scenario to solve the problem: *"Let me jump my battery with another to see if it's my battery that's bad."* Presto, logical thinking did solve that problem, and it may solve another now that it can reflect on an understanding gained in the past.

In seeking solutions to problems, we often encourage the internal monologue of thought streaming because it appears similar and related to our past success with logical thinking. Example: *"I fixed my car because I remembered all the problems I had starting cars in* the past. *I'll bet if I remember the problems I had with all my past girlfriends, I can fix the problem I have now with Suzie.*" However, this approach is a significant error in the use of our mental processes.

Our internal monologue may begin with "*I wonder if I should change my behavior with Suzie.*" The mental monologue typically continues to sift through scenario after scenario, searching for an answer, yet no real solution appears: "*I wonder if I should give her more flowers. Perhaps I should wear red socks. My mom likes them.*" The ruminations feed upon themselves, with the ones currently active in our consciousness encouraging subsequent ones. As thought streaming continues without a solution, our frustration builds because we mistakenly believe that we're using the right process to find our answer.

As I've already pointed out, thought streaming doesn't help us solve problems. In the example with Suzie, maybe this young woman understands that her personality doesn't fit with his. The young man tries to use logic and thought streaming to solve his relationship problems when he really needs to have an insight about their mutual personality differences. There's also a second problem: Because thought streaming doesn't help solve problems, it actually causes anxiety. Consider how anxious this young man must feel. Because he can't find a solution to his problem through thought streaming, despite the expenditure of a lot of mental energy, he begins to feel hopeless.

Such hopelessness often brings with it a strong emotional component, such as sadness, worthlessness, or frustration. These feelings drain us of our happiness and cause us much discontent. It's best, therefore, to stay away from thought streaming if you want to solve problems and avoid such intense negative emotions as sadness, anxiety, and worthlessness.

HOW INDIVIDUAL THOUGHTS CAN DEVELOP INTO STREAMS

Individual thoughts come up into consciousness for us all the time. No one knows why, and no one knows whether they have any meaning. Various people I know have reported some of their individual thoughts to me as centering around the following ideas:

- Adopting more cats
- Striking an infant child
- Sharing true feelings with a boss
- Buying an extravagant car
- Having an extramarital affair
- Needing more jewelry in order to look better
- Being a voiceover actor in a Disney animation feature
- Leaving home and family in order to take on a completely new life in another more exciting country
- Becoming a vegetarian
- Disliking an ethnic, social, or religious group

As individual thoughts arise, we may see them as the random generation of nerve activity that they probably are. Each of the thoughts listed above may give birth to a thought stream. Down what streams will these individual thoughts go, and to what end? Will thought streams about cats, adoptions, or luxury cars help us in living? I can say with certainty that they will not. As to the timing or process of their arising, I don't believe anyone knows when they'll come or what their content will be. We must cope with the fact of life that they arise, and we must choose what to do with them. We need not encourage individual thoughts to continue into thought streams. If we do encourage individual occurrences of thought— even those that seem trivial—we risk encouraging our general tendency to thought stream.

An In-depth Look at Thought Streaming

Levels of Thought Streaming

From our own experience, we know that all thought streaming isn't equal. Some thought streaming creates tremendous struggle within us. Here's an example: *"I've busted my butt at work to get this promotion. I really need the money that comes with it so Andy can continue with school. That somebody else got the job just sticks in my craw. He's often late to work, and his overly kind attention to the boss certainly isn't genuine."* This kind of thought streaming is notorious for keeping us awake at night and distracted from our work during the day. Here's another example of thought streaming, which does little more than disturb our inner mental clarity: *"I hope JoAnn likes me. We had a fine time at dinner last night."* Because the strength of our thought streaming varies considerably, I find it useful to make distinctions among their levels of difficulty. In order of increasing intensity and problematic nature, these levels include the *Placid Pool*, the *Simple Stream*, the *Rushing River*, and the *Toxic Torrent*.

The first level, the Placid Pool, is really not a level at all, since thought streaming is absent. It happens often with us, but we may not notice it because it's characterized by a lack of thought streaming. We experience the Placid Pool during or just after strenuous exercise, during meditation, when knitting or crocheting with good concentration, when first stumbling out of bed in the morning, and when giving someone our undivided attention. We enjoy this state of mind, and we want to get it back when it leaves. The Placid Pool is what feels so good about knitting a sweater or receiving someone's undivided attention. The great feeling of our own basic aliveness appears when thought streaming doesn't block it.

The second level, the Simple Stream, is typically characterized by sporadic or repeated thoughts that don't have much emotional charge to them. Thought streams such as "Milk, milk, I need to get milk at the store," lyrics from catchy songs like *Lose Yourself* or *The Lion Sleeps Tonight*, and popular phrases from TV ads exemplify Simple Streams that clog consciousness.

These thought streams present little problem in our daily life, especially when compared to those that prevent us from sleeping or that keep us in a state of rage against someone. Still, I consider Simple Streams to be the most serious offenders because they are constantly with us, blocking our intimacy with the world. Have you ever talked on a cell phone with someone who was driving his car? The driver needs to split attention between you and the road. When the driver does this, he can't talk intimately. He can set a date to meet you but can't help you untangle more difficult issues, such as complicated problems at work, because he can't give you the focused attention you need.

Simple Streams are similar. They fragment our attention from conversing well with others, focusing on a business deal, or reviewing a sheet full of calculations or financial numbers. Basically, Simple Streams separate us from our lives, yet we can easily stop them once we've noticed them (which is the hardest part of the process). With that accomplished, we can wake up from their trance fairly easy. I encourage everyone to work diligently on stopping Simple Streams. Beginning practice in this area can have the most tangible and beneficial results in your life. When you learn to stop or discourage Simple Streams, you'll develop a mental clarity that will help you in the widest range of daily events. This simple practice can yield great results.

When thought streaming presents a more acute problem in our life, it rises to the third level, the Rushing River. Here persistent thought streams characterize our mental monologue. These thought streams also have a significant interest or emotionality about them.

Because these two properties—persistency and interest or emotionality—have combined, Rushing Rivers are tenacious. We have a much more difficult time stopping or discouraging them because they have become problems in and of themselves. Rushing Rivers like the following example keep us on edge: "Oh, *the repairman forgot to check with his car muffler supplier, so he couldn't fix my car today as promised. Now I'm stuck at home and will miss a meeting that could help settle our year-end finances. How could he forget—and on a day as important as this one!*" This kind of thought streaming causes anxiety, makes us focus on negativity, imprisons us in our own limited point of view, and leads us to the hasty generalization that the entire car-repair industry is inept.

With some effort, we can stop Rushing Rivers. As with stopping Simple Streams, we first have to notice that we've entered a Rushing River. However, they can so insidiously envelop us that we don't even know we're in one. Once we've noticed that we're caught in a Rushing River of thought streaming, we can't always immediately free ourselves from it. If we can stop one, great! If it won't stop right away, we need to promise ourselves we'll stop it or distract ourselves from it sooner or later. We just need to keep up the effort. If we can distract ourselves by turning our attention to another matter, great! People often find relief from Rushing Rivers by working in the garden, reading a book, washing dishes, exercising, or doing other activities that require attention. Sometimes we can stop or distract ourselves from Rushing Rivers immediately, but other times require sustained effort. The important thing is to keep trying.

The fourth level of thought streaming, the Toxic Torrent, is the most difficult to work with. Thankfully, we encounter it only at times of unusual distress. At this level, thought streaming is incessant and plagued by great interest or emotionality. Often, we easily notice that we're in a Toxic Torrent because we're extremely angry or sad. We may experience disruptions in our sleeping and eating patterns and in our relationships. Clearly, we know we're upset. How difficult it is to stop or distract ourselves from Toxic Torrents like the following: *"There are rumors of a big layoff at work and just after we move into our first house. Maybe we won't be able to make payments on it. Damn! Starting a family in a cramped apartment is no way to live. We had to move out. Now what will we do?"*

With practice in stopping or distracting ourselves from less problematic thought streaming, we begin to build the capability of stopping the most difficult ones. At times, Toxic Torrents are difficult to stop because we believe they're beneficial. We believe, *"Why shouldn't I worry about my house, my pregnant wife, and our financial health as a family? I'm supposed to worry about this."* Until we have the insight that thought streaming doesn't help us solve problems (that is, until we resolve the primary error of thought streaming), we'll continue to encourage our own needless worry. A mind full of worried thoughts doesn't have the mental clarity required to find the best solutions to problems. Such a mind only incapacitates the owner with anxiety.

The techniques of stopping or distracting ourselves from Toxic Torrents are the same ones we use for Rushing Rivers. Clearly, these require more effort to silence. Yet we can completely silence them or drop our fascination with them, so they don't grab our attention if we undertake constant practice. Take a moment to imagine what your life would be like if Toxic Torrents never gained control of your mind. Even if you had a terrible problem, like a job loss or a beloved family member's illness, Toxic Torrents wouldn't harm you. You would handle the problem with intelligence and care, in large part because the Toxic Torrent itself would be missing.

THE CENTRAL POINT OF THIS BOOK

This book urges readers to examine how thought streams affect the quality of their daily lives. In my personal experience, I have found that thought streams are:

1. Quite unnecessary for us to make our way in the world.
2. Volitional in that we passively decide to allow them to occur.
3. Actually harmful during the conduct of our daily lives.
4. Best discouraged as quickly as we can (even those that seem positive).

I hope this book helps you understand the high cost you pay in not investigating the primary errors involved in logical thinking and thought streaming. When you resolve these errors and misconceptions, you can develop a more mature and beneficial form of mental functioning that uses reflection in conjunction with logical thinking. At the same time, you won't become overly fascinated or caught up by thought streaming. When you acknowledge the limits of logical thinking and recognize the harm caused by thought streaming, you have the opportunity to change the ways in which you solve problems. Instead of trying in vain to find logical answers to intractable problems, you can seek to encourage insights. To do this requires dropping your mental monologue and learning to reflect on a problem instead.

While reflection is a difficult process to describe, we can characterize it by a lack of mental monologue. Yet when we keep a problem "in mind," in open awareness, insights will come.

A MATURATIONAL MODEL

Here's a model that describes a mature view of mental processes: Basic Awareness —> Thought Occurs—> Logical Thinking

Occurs—> The Primary Error About Logical Thinking Occurs —> Thought Streaming Occurs —> The Primary Error About Thought Streaming Occurs —> The Primary Errors About Logical Thinking and Thought Streaming Are Resolved —> Reflection Occurs.

Let me explain this process in some depth. When we're very young, from the time we're newborn until probably the time we develop speech (usually at age two), our consciousness, which is rather primitive, develops rapidly. We have basic awareness; that is, our five senses are intact, but our consciousness is immature. We can't speak and probably can't use thought processes of any sort.

Although it's hard to know for sure, we can reasonably posit that we begin to express ourselves in speech when we're neurologically mature enough to have instances of thought. I don't know of any research on when we can or do first have thoughts, yet I believe they arise when we first begin to speak. From then on, we can verbally express that we have hunger or some other need. Whenever the process starts, thoughts arise into consciousness spontaneously, and this activity continues throughout our lifetime.

Following the initial occurrence of thought, we subsequently learn about logical thinking. Most of us learn the rules of language and the equally complex rules of arithmetic and mathematics. Many of us learn other formal rules of logic, such as those for inference and derivation, and try to apply those rules to the world.

Typically, we then overestimate the capabilities of logical thinking, believing it so powerful as to be useful in all situations; this is the primary error about logical thinking. Many of us believe that logic can solve the world's most intractable problems. In time, this belief won't bear itself out as true. We need to leap beyond logic into insight to solve the problems that chronically plague us.

By giving free rein to a mental process that's incapable of actually solving problems, we make the all-too-common primary error about thought streaming. Although we may dramatically increase our degree of mental monologue, solutions to our problems won't appear. Not knowing what else to do and apparently having no other options, we continue our thought streaming in the hope of finding answers.

Yet in doing this, we seriously underestimate the harm that thought streaming causes in our lives. In the next chapter, I'll discuss the negative impact of thought streaming.

When we have insights, solutions to our most difficult problems appear spontaneously. Yes, at times logical thinking can give us the answers to certain problems. However, we mustn't forget that we have two tools to support us in life: logical thinking and reflection. In coming to this understanding, we resolve both the primary errors of thinking and thought streaming. When we appropriately use logical thinking and reflection as the need requires, we have the flexibility to find the answers we need to manage our lives successfully and happily in this complex world.

TRY THIS:

E V E R Y once in a while when you're *not* sitting quietly, but going for a walk, vacuuming a carpet, or sweeping with a broom, look at your thoughts.

A S K yourself three things about the thoughts that stream on: *Are you having many or a few of them? Are they helpful to you? Are they important to have in mind to live a better life?*

Y O U don't need to sit quietly to examine your thought streaming, but it's useful when you're just beginning to look at them. Now that you can see them, what's your opinion of them? Are they helpful and necessary, or are they trivial and often worrisome?

CHAPTER SEVEN

Styles of Thought Streaming

"The happiness of your life depends upon the quality of your thoughts."
—Marcus Aurelius

I'VE identified a number of common thought streaming "styles," which I'll describe shortly. They manifest not only during relatively high-velocity thought streaming, but also at times of average speed. Furthermore, these styles describe the ways in which we use and unwittingly direct thought streams when we don't know how to work with them properly or control them through practice.

I've identified five prominent styles, but there may be more. I developed a sense of common thought streaming styles by keeping my ear attuned to *how* people were speaking, rather than listening to the meaning of their words. Have you ever noticed that regardless of what some people say, they tend to be argumentative? Don't some people often just ramble on as they speak, hardly ever getting to a significant conclusion? Because these styles of speaking reflect the mental monologue from which their speech originates, they represent styles of thought streaming.

I'm not sure that my list of styles is complete, but a complete list isn't necessary. By describing common styles, I've shown that even our streams of thought have a tendency to cluster and organize themselves to respond in a stereotypical manner. This clustering decreases our ability to consider new views or fresh ideas. When we become conscious of becoming stuck in a certain style, we have a better chance of seeing its limitations and changing our perspective to one that might offer a wider, more helpful view.

WHAT IS YOUR OWN THOUGHT STREAMING STYLE?

The following short quiz will help you identify your own style or styles of thought streaming. Please look at the five sentences below and rank them according to your affinity with them. Assign a score of five to the statement that describes the type of thought you most commonly have, and a four, three, two, and one to the statements that describes the types of thought you least commonly have.

A. You have concerns about specific issues and feel compelled to examine them thoroughly from a variety of angles.

B. An escape to a distant destination, full of folklore and history, strongly entices you.

C. Your thoughts breezily move on from one topic to another (e.g., lunch, kids, work tasks, shopping).

D. You wish the members of your family would let you know what they're doing right now.

E. The craftsmanship or orderliness around your house could be better.

Which statements did you rank as numbers five and four? These are your top two thought streaming styles. Statement A relates to a Wondering style of thought streaming; B relates to a Fantasizing style; C relates to a Wandering style; D relates to a Checking style; and E relates to a Critiquing style. No one uses just one style, and because each category is somewhat variable, they tend to overlap. I believe we can all benefit from a careful look at styles of thought streaming, which I'll describe in some detail.

We can use these descriptions to become more familiar with the unconscious ways in which we approach the world. When we use any particular style, we artificially structure how we perceive and react to the world around us. If we don't consistently use one particular style, or we don't use any style at all, we approach the world with more flexibility, better prepared to handle what comes our way.

THOUGHT STREAMING AS A PSYCHOLOGICAL DEFENSE

People have asked me whether these thought streaming styles represent some sort of psychological defense. I don't believe they operate that way. I believe, instead, that these styles reflect the variety of an individual's basic traits and life circumstances, which may solidify and be used more frequently, thus becoming a habit pattern or thought streaming style. Yet as far as psychological defenses are concerned, I don't think these styles are that deeply formed.

However, regardless of the style employed, the act of thought streaming constitutes a psychological defense. Consider a difficulty that you don't wish to face. Usually, real-life scenarios that are simply contrary to one of our wishes or beliefs cause difficulties.

For example, we may be threatened by a potential layoff at work. Apart from the financial threat to self and family, this situation poses a real threat to our self-image of being capable, valuable, and able to control our life. It also threatens our identity as a particular type of worker (whether we work at automobile assembly, sell high-end clothing, or style hair). To maintain our fixed notions of being capable, valuable, and in control, while at the same time facing a job layoff, something has to help us defend our untenable position. Enter the psychological defense.

Thought streaming appears to help us defend our position. If we falsely believe that thinking helps us solve problems, we commit the primary error about thought streaming. Similarly, if we believe that thought streaming is related to logical thinking, we commit the primary error in that regard, and we go into thought streaming. The more mental noise we make, the more we obscure the real problem.

Say, for example, that a job layoff looms, and we truly can't control it. The closer we get to the time of the layoff, the more mental material we may harbor as we consider one view of the situation after another. We may simply fantasize about suing the company, or we may scheme about showing the company how valuable and in control we really are. We may think, *"I'll show them. I'm a great worker. I'll bet I can get the union to file a class action complaint. They can't do this to the working man."* Our thought streaming may so intensify that we imagine scenarios in which others targeted for layoff join us in showing the company our collective value.

But, in fact, the job layoff may be completely out of our control, as well as the control of management. It may have little or no relationship to our true value and capability; larger economic forces may be at work. Yet we may mentally scheme to prove our point. Because of our personal belief system, we hope to show others our high value, capability, state of control, and affiliation with the group in which we work. We hope others won't see us as the average, typical person we are.

When we practice stopping thought streaming, these psychological defenses and thought streaming styles can and do drop away. As we view the relevance of our thoughts more realistically, and we see that the vast majority of them are unnecessary and that streams of them are actually harmful, thoughts drop off in their frequency. At the same time that the number of our thoughts decreases, thought streaming styles drop, too. The foundation for this style of thought streaming collapses, since the thought streams themselves have gone.

THE PRESENCE OF ANY STYLE IS A SURE INDICATOR OF THOUGHT STREAMING

As I describe styles of thought streaming, you'll notice that the one that best describes yours includes some of the characteristics of every other style. That's because the styles are not narrow or restrictive. You can have different styles at different times, and often they mix together.

You may wonder whether any of these styles is at all useful. I've observed that *none* of them is useful. Each occurs according to our natural tendencies when thought streaming is up and running. While these styles aren't useful, we may nonetheless see them as indicators of being in the midst of unnecessary thought streaming. Perhaps you may notice them in yourself; they may give you cues about your own thought-streaming episodes.

Conversely, we may view the dropping of thought streaming as an indicator of psychological health. As I suggested above, if we use thought streaming as a psychological defense, then dropping it coincides with dropping psychological defensiveness. Normally, we enlist defenses to support a fixed position for ourselves, supporting our felt sense that we are one way or another (kind, smart, strong, mean, controlling, or angry). When we're willing to drop these fixed notions about ourself by stopping our thought streaming, we lessen our defensiveness and open ourselves to the possibility of existing more fully and flexibly in the world.

Critiquing

Critiquing, the first thought streaming style, involves engaging in a running commentary on the quality of our experience or its apparent lack. We continually evaluate the performance either of ourself, another person, or a situation.

One example of the critiquing style involves self-directed mental interjections. We say disparaging things to ourselves such as, *"Boy, that was a goofy thing I said,"* or we might comment sarcastically, *"Nice going!"* These comments, directed inward, are characteristically derisive and self-demeaning in nature.

When we critique other people or events, we often direct our critical thoughts outward. If these thoughts demean others, we may disparage them as "lazy" or "incompetent," whether they actually possess these traits or not. In general, people with a love for fashion appreciate the critiquing style and direct their commentary to the many fashion targets in the world. Reporters of fashion on television feel free to verbally critique people who have apparently mismatched colors, shapes, or accessories. Many of us only mentally critique others.

Viewers who watch aspiring singers vie for idol status on television get into a critiquing style while the show is on. Typically, they make critical comments on vocal pitch, song tempo, and difficulty, as well as a myriad of other factors.

I notice this style in my friends when they're watching sports. In fact, I sometimes think that my friends enjoy spectator sports mainly to expose their critiquing style safely in one of its more appropriate settings. Whatever the sport—tennis, baseball, surfing, football, soccer, or basketball—some people continually evaluate athletes' performances during competitive games where scores are kept and winners and losers are assigned.

One good friend of mine enjoys "scoring the game" through the box score in baseball. This fellow listens to Los Angeles Dodgers games on the radio. The announcer comments on whether the ball was hit or not, who caught and threw it, and where it went during each play of the game. These descriptions give my friend ample opportunity to critique "that bum of an outfielder," "the worst choice for a designated hitter by any manager in baseball history," and so on. Hours often go by like this, filled with one negative comment after another. Even if the Dodgers win the game, my friend simply believes that luck has intervened.

My friend's usual style of thought streaming changes when he listens to a game. A consistent and wandering parade of thoughts keeps his mind occupied throughout most of his activities, but at a more moderate pace. However, when baseball comes on the radio or TV, his thought streaming becomes as rapid and critical as anyone I've ever seen. Just what is the benefit?

Checking

The next thought streaming style, checking, consists of engaging in an internal monologue in which we attempt to determine whether things are going according to some vague plan. In the checking style, we may see whether things are satisfactory or whether people are satisfied. This style shows itself most commonly in a stepwise manner as we check whether things live up to our expectation at this time and whether they'll continue to do so as things unfold according to our inner mental "plan."

Some internal monologues of this type feature continuous

checking to see whether people are having a good time. Similarly, we may check on other people's response to us or run a commentary about whether things are on schedule. When we engage in checking behavior, we make comparisons between past experience and future expectations. For example, we'll remember an excellent meal that we had in the past and cling to the expectation that the next meal must measure up to this standard. We engage in a moment-to-moment examination to evaluate whether the current situation meets our often rigid expectations.

My favorite example of the checking style involves someone who went to the beach with friends to see the sunset. This person didn't really get to see it because she continually checked on her friends to determine whether they were having a good time and not fighting with each other. In addition, she checked on whether the temperature was warm enough and the breeze wasn't too cool. Her thought streaming went something like this: *"I wonder if it was a good idea to organize this trip to the beach to watch the sunset. Is Gail happy? She doesn't seem to be. I wonder if she's too cold. Pat and Nancy aren't talking much. I wonder if they're arguing again or if they're just too cold."*

The checking thought-streaming style throws a curtain of thought between us and the objective world, filtering intimacy and reality by whatever content happens to arise. Consider this scenario: Two women are viewing a lovely, colorful sunset. One woman, who sees the event unfiltered by thought streaming, experiences an orange sun, a red sky, and deep blue water; she smells the salt air and feels a fresh breeze. The other misses the beauty of the sunset because thought streaming about the cold, the wind, and a dispute with a friend dominates her awareness. Who would you rather be?

Now the question arises: How involved are you in thought

streaming? Reflect on your own daily activities. Are you present for the important matters of life, like sunsets, work duties, and personal encounters? Or do you have a lot in common with the woman who thought streamed her way out of enjoying a beautiful sunset?

Wandering

In the wandering style, what we usually call daydreaming or being lost in thought typifies thought streams. In this style, our thoughts jump randomly from one topic to another. We relate to topics only loosely; one word or sound triggers a new thought somehow related to it. We often use this style as entertainment, although most people wouldn't admit to using it that way. We may also generate thoughts voluntarily to keep the mind occupied. In other words, if our thoughts trail off, we come up with new thoughts and create a thought streaming session from this new beginning. This style often dominates our consciousness whenever we're bored; hence, I call it entertainment.

Here's an example from my own life that comes from the past. When I'd be nearing the end of a workday, I'd sometimes feel bored because I had little to do. I couldn't efficiently begin another project because the day would soon be coming to a close. A stream of thoughts would start, beginning with the observation that it was nearly time to leave work. I might then think about my car, which wasn't in the best mechanical condition. This thought would segué into one about my own mechanical condition (my own health), and this in turn would change into a thought about my needing to eat more vegetables, and on it would go, a parade of thoughts that entertained me while I waited for the workday to end.

People who await the results of critical laboratory tests, like those of biopsies for cancer, can easily enter a wandering style of thought streaming. Their thoughts might jump from their general health status to why they may get cancer while others avoid it, to whether taking vitamins and exercising would keep them cancer-free. Other thought streams may include random musings such as, *"I'm concerned that Marie is sad about me. I wish I could repair my relationship with my father so I don't die with that anger. I remember that weekend vacation at the beach where we all had a great time playing games of horseshoes."*

As with other styles of thought streaming, wandering keeps your attention away from present reality. You may be bored or you may seek to distance yourself from some undesirable emotion. You may be underutilized at your job, or some other factor may bring about the feeling of boredom. However the boredom has developed, you want to avoid the feeling, and you can do that cheaply and effectively by initiating some entertaining thoughts. You may not do this on purpose, yet you may be so accustomed to calling on thought streams to ease your boredom that they appear with little or no encouragement.

Wondering

The person who uses the wondering style encourages thoughts of the future in "what if" planning scenarios. I like to compare wondering-style thinkers to soap opera watchers. When we find our thought scenes entertaining like soap operas, each scene leaves room for inquiry into another "what if" scenario.

Here's a general example of a wondering thought stream: *"I wonder what the result will be if something happens in this particular way or that particular way. If it happens the first way, a certain result will follow, but if it happens the second way, a different outcome will result."*

When I was in college, a group of friends and I watched the

movie *A Night to Remember*, which is about the sinking of the *Titanic* on her maiden voyage. At the coffee shop afterward, a man and woman in our group were chatting about the movie, especially about fate. The conversation went along these lines: *"What if the Titanic had been delayed? Would it have missed the iceberg? If it had missed the iceberg, would have been sunk during the war? If it had been a hospital ship, would it have avoided being sunk in the war?"*

This discussion went on in a lively fashion for a good fifteen minutes while the rest of us listened. The two speakers kept contributing to the conversation with "what if" scenarios that rose to a crescendo of increasing improbability. Their speculation included the Titanic's being delayed from departing, sinking from a torpedo shot by a submarine, and being used as a hospital ship during the war.

This conversation about the Titanic serves as a good example of what occurs in the wondering thought streaming style. The topic makes no difference; in this instance, it happened to be a movie. Clearly, thought streaming occurs because we haven't trained our minds to do otherwise. No class in our system of formal education teaches us to corral the wanderings of our mind. Thus, we use it for entertainment and as a filter that distances or obscures the reality that confronts us.

The two people talking about the Titanic weren't trying to get to know each other. Their conversation acted more like a screening blockade and attempt to hold center stage than a back-and-forth discussion or any attempt to establish common ground.

At this point, a brief reminder is in order. This couple was practicing the encouragement of thought streaming, which has detrimental effects, the foremost being that we don't learn to stop this runaway mental process. We practice discouraging our thought streaming because we want some peace of mind or because we need concentration to read and understand a book. If we don't learn to corral our wandering mind, we'll have more problems than those who have practiced reining in their thoughts.

Fantasizing

The thought streaming style I call *fantasizing* is much like the wondering style, except that it encourages thoughts that are more escapist, magical, or outlandish than those we find in our usual daily life. Examples come from realms of the unusual, like the following fanciful stream: *"What if I marry a rich person? We could afford to have two homes. If they were in different countries, I wonder if our children would speak more than one language."*

People who use this style think about the mysteries of elves, invisible worlds, and the personification of inanimate objects such as trees. These people, who are not delusional or otherwise psychotic, have a strong affinity for things fantastic. Their thought streams take into account forces that are hidden to the eye, such as the following example: *"The energy of trees makes it difficult for grass to grow under them, and that grass has healing powers when made into tea. However, the tea loses its power if it's consumed cold."* Such thoughts are eccentric, but not sick. Still, this style of thought streaming is as unhealthy as any other.

In fact, fantasizing may offer people the imagined benefit of experiencing the unusual and standing out from their peers. For this reason, they may wish to keep thought streaming in this way without understanding the true cost of keeping up this unrealistic style—or any other, for that matter. Once we start thought streaming, it's easy to continue doing it. We can analyze a situation, analyze the analysis, analyze the analysis of the analysis, and so on, ad infinitum. In the end, we've acquired no incremental understanding, even though we've brought a great deal of "thought" to the challenge. What good does it all do? Actually, it simply does harm and no good at all.

MIND GAMES

To finish our discussion, I would like to correlate thought streams with a popular phenomenon in our culture known as *mind games*. This isn't a fully formed style, but it's a thought streaming strategy that is frequently used.

I define a mind game as the thoughts accompanying mental speculation about interpersonal relationships. We may initiate a mind game, for example, when we don't understand why a friend's anger triggers anger in us or when we complete a telephone call with another friend feeling confused by comments he made about our appearance. When we play mind games, we speculate about possible reasons for our friend's anger (perhaps he lost his job, was betrayed by a friend, or was the victim of credit card fraud). If the speculation rambles on and if it draws unwarranted conclusions, as it often does because it lacks true and basic information, the speculator has had a bit of entertainment, often at the expense of the person with the problem. In this way, a small harm has developed.

THE DESTRUCTIVENESS OF MIND GAMES

Like all other thought streaming patterns, seemingly innocent mind games are ultimately destructive. They represent one of the more harmful uses of thought streaming because the psychological abuse they engender typically harms an innocent party, the person who is the object of the thoughts.

Mind games, which are essentially dramatic soap operas, often develop unwittingly at first. The interpersonal scenarios *appear* to help the mind gamer's self-esteem because they often relate to interpretations of events that could *possibly* be true. Here's an example of a young man engaged in a romantic mind game: *"If I tell Elaine that I like Patty, maybe Elaine will feel jealous and will want to be with me more. I don't really like Patty because she didn't invite me to her party. I really wanted to go with Elaine."* Mind gamers may speculate on how best to injure others psychologically without being identified; how best to arrange personal circumstances to get what they desire; how to look inferior or superior in ways others must acknowledge; or how to show that others are better or not as good as they are.

The scenarios we create are either relatively improbable or, in fact, impossible. Mind gamers use created dramas based on mental speculation about personal relationships to avoid real-life situations or to entertain themselves during times of boredom or unhappiness. More often than not, mind game thought streaming harms both the perpetrator and the objects of their scenarios.

WE'RE BETTER OFF WITH NO THOUGHT STREAMING STYLE

I'm not suggesting that the thought streaming styles I've described are the only ones. They simply represent styles I've observed in people subject to incessant thought streaming. Actually, we can become involved in many types of thought content and produce an interesting array of chronic mental behavior.

Generally, we need a large volume of thoughts produced over a lengthy period of time for a thought streaming style to continue. As we practice and achieve a lack of interest in our own thought streaming, the various styles also tend to cease. For example, if you're prone to the fantasizing style but have dramatically reduced your thought load, the mental support for this style will cease. When a predominant style is gone, people react more appropriately to what's happening in their lives. With their thought streaming reduced, a strongly influential mental process no longer prejudices them. Now they have a better life, one that includes peace of mind, the ability to pay good attention, and appropriate ways to interact with others.

FREE YOUR MIND

CHAPTER EIGHT

Harm From Thought Streaming

"A crust eaten in peace is better than a banquet partaken in anxiety."
—Aesop

N O W that we've identified common thought streaming styles, let's explore specific ways in which thought streaming actually harms us and impairs our daily functioning. As you read about these seven main areas, please linger over them a bit. In each category, I'll offer a few descriptions about the harmful effects of thought streaming. Some will apply to you directly, others only indirectly. Don't fool yourself that these examples are only situations of potential harm. As you look into the seven types of harm caused by thought streaming, consider how they apply to your own life.

1. Anxiety and the Disruption of Activities

The central tenet of this book is that thought streams *cause* anxiety and disrupt our activities. This idea may go against our usual beliefs until we examine them carefully.

Many of us experience "earworms," as they're called—those bothersome, catchy phrases or commercial jingles that won't leave our mind even when we try to banish them. They ramble on repetitively, often with bits of songs. For example, when we're invaded by *The Lion Sleeps Tonight*, we hear the phrase, *"In the jungle, the quiet jungle . . ."* These repetitive catch phrases may come from song lyrics or from subtle messages that we unconsciously say to ourselves. We also may get stuck in mental chatter that says, *"I'm unworthy. They'll hate me if I do what I want to do. I'm angry at my boss."*

These mental sound bites bother us because they obscure our experience with a screen of thought streaming. They impede our concentration on matters to which we would like to attend. A screen of thoughts keeps us from concentrating on enjoyable reading, personal conversations, and high-quality work on the job.

Even if the catch phrase is seemingly neutral, like part of a nice song, the blockading of our attention causes a generalized form of anxiety. We feel out of control when these thought streams occur against our will. Because we want to be in control of our thoughts and actions, we become anxious and frustrated that these thought streams won't go away when we want them to.

This anxiety is further heightened when we need to concentrate to perform some task. An eye surgeon trying to focus on a patient's cataract will experience considerable anxiety when interfering thoughts disrupt her concentration. A father trying to teach a child to read will feel similar anxiety when unwanted thought streaming content (such as his shopping list, a conflict at work, or concerns about his mother-in-law) distract him from this important task. A golfer can't putt, a reader can't read, a writer can't write, an inspector can't inspect, and a chess player can't make a move until mental distractions subside. I just know that my golf buddy hums a few bars from *The Lion Sleeps Tonight* as we roll down the fairway to the next hole so that the song will enter my mind and distract me from good putting!

All these examples—serious and otherwise—show how frustrated we become when we're mentally hampered from doing something well. We also feel frustrated when we can't get right to sleep because our thoughts are bothering us, when we feel continuing resentment toward our parents for alleged past abuse, or when our thoughts assail us with a sense of worthlessness. At these times, thought streaming presents a pernicious obstacle to our well-being.

In addition, thought streaming itself causes anxiety. Most of us understand that anxiety causes anxious thoughts. When a situation develops that we don't like, we look for a solution. When a solution isn't readily available, we begin to thought stream about it. In this sequence of events, thought streaming is a symptom of anxiety. Yet the opposite is also true.

Because thought streaming invades our consciousness, blocks our attention, and becomes an unwanted and seemingly permanent aspect of our mental processes, it also *causes* anxiety. The hallmark of anxiety is chronic worry, and what is worry if not our own thought streaming on the topics of past, present, or future problems? We all have problems for which solutions aren't readily available. However, as I pointed out before, thought streaming can't help us find the answers to significant problems; only insight can.

If we were to stop thought streaming, could we still have anxiety? In a word, the answer is no. We could have an initial, appropriate concern about a problem, but for this concern to linger as worry, thought streaming would have to carry it on in time. Without thought streaming, it would simply become one of the many problems in our life that gets solved when the time is right.

Although there are many things we can worry about, death and public speaking always appear high on the list. Thought streaming about death causes us to worry about the possibility of future pain, our salvation, and our family's grief once we're gone. How does worry help us solve these problems? Thought streaming about speaking in front of an audience causes us to worry about reactions to our intelligence and physical appearance. How does worry help us speak publicly? We don't solve our problems about death and public speaking by thought streaming about them. While we all will go through these problems at some time in our lives, adding worry to these realities only makes life miserable. Stopping or becoming disentangled in thought streaming prevents adding unwanted, unnecessary misery to these situations and makes life much more joyful.

When thought streaming carries a problem, such as public speaking, forward in time, it changes it into a chronic concern or worry. Can we stop thought streaming? Yes, we certainly can, although we can't stop individual bursts of single thought. If we can stop thought streaming, why don't we? Perhaps we never considered the possibility, or we mistakenly believe that we need thought streams to get though daily life. If we correct this misperception, we'll all lead much happier lives.

2. A DECREASE IN INTIMACY
Thought streams can run through our minds with high energy and high speed, low energy and low speed, or some combination of both. However they appear, they intrude into our consciousness, and the sooner we clear it of this mental refuse, the better off we'll be.

Do you remember the example of the father who experienced incessant thought streaming while trying to teach his child to read? Without a doubt, this father will feel a lack of intimacy in the process. When I've worked in clinics that help adults become better parents, I've seen both men and women facing the same problem. Thought streams place a barrier between the world and us. How can we help children read when we can't keep our own attention on the book? Thought streaming doesn't allow us direct interaction with a child or another adult, and, naturally, this interferes with intimacy.

Without intimacy, we miss the opportunity to fully understand what a person is trying to communicate to us, as well as the entire situation that's presently unfolding. A parent may miss the fact that his child can't see as clearly as other children. Words may appear blurry, causing an obvious problem for the child. However, the child's father may not recognize this problem because of his own mental preoccupation with problems at his workplace. His ability to respond to his child's needs may be obscured by thoughts like these: *"Joan and Jack are both up for promotion, and I've only got one slot. Both would be great taking on more responsibility. Jack has been with the company longer, but Joan has equal experience. One is Native American and the other is Hispanic, so there's no problem with perceptions of racial bias."*

Sometimes our mental preoccupations come with prejudices that further decrease our intimacy with a situation. The screen of streaming thoughts prevents us from becoming emotionally close enough to understand other people. This separation, which decreases our humanness, makes us see others as objects instead of human beings. If we treat them as objects, we care less whether they're hungry, cold, thirsty, suffering, or otherwise miserable. Without thought streaming, we're better than this; we're more fully human.

Thought streaming actually can blind us to our life. It throws a curtain of thought between us and the objective world. Filtering all direct experience through whatever concern happens to arise, thought streaming can cause us to miss the entirety of our life experiences.

When thought streaming is out of control, we profoundly miss even the intimacy with ourselves and our special loved ones that we could otherwise experience. We seek sports, hobbies, and vacations to regain the intimacy with the self that's been lost due to mental intrusions. Our teeming thoughts screen us from the basic aliveness that we appreciate so much when we're in contact with it. We truly value this aliveness; just look at the expense we'll incur for recreation designed to get ourselves back in touch with it! If we had access to this basic aliveness on a daily basis—and this certainly happens when thought streaming is reduced—we would feel a wonderful new fulfillment and satisfaction. And think of the money we'd save!

3. USELESS (IF NOT HARMFUL) SPECULATION

Another potential harm from uncontrolled thought streaming comes from speculation. While speculation includes mind games based on interpersonal relationships, in broader terms it involves mental activity in which we ponder the unknowable without using logic or action to find real answers. Such speculation distracts us and leads us away from other activities—compassionate ones, for instance, that would enhance our own and other people's lives.

We can easily identify examples of speculative thought streaming. Are there canals on Mars that brought water to a great civilization? Do ghosts inhabit the earth? Can curses cause people harm? Are intelligent extraterrestrials at the controls of UFOs? Does life continue after bodily death?

I don't oppose studying such questions, but prolonged mental rambling adds energy to thinking that's already unrealistic and takes us further away from our immediate reality. When we use logic to plan a long bridge or design a spacecraft to carry the latest instruments, we receive real benefits from such mental activity.

What good has speculative thought streaming ever done? None! Probably its most significant harm comes from its promotion of thought streaming itself. Even though it has no basis in logic, we let our minds wander toward the fantastic. By encouraging this speculation, we find it difficult to stop personally damaging thoughts when we want or need to.

We also harm ourselves by spending time on fruitless matters that we can't know, instead of on practical matters that directly lead to happiness and productivity. If we feel strongly about some creative topic, we might best take some non-mental action. James "The Amazing" Randi provides a good example of this. He was interested in magic, and after a good deal of practice, he became an excellent magician. As a young man, he probably speculated about how magicians perform their greatest tricks. Finally, he took action and actually learned the trade. Later in life, he became one of the greatest skeptics regarding magic. From my point of view, the Amazing Randi turned the penchant he may have had for unproductive mental speculation (thought streaming) into an enjoyable career that also brings happiness to others.

Here are some well-known yet highly questionable speculations held by seemingly normal people who couldn't constrain their thought streaming:

- "The Earth is the center of the universe" (see pre-Copernican philosophers and religious thinkers).
- "There are witches with supernatural powers" (see the Inquisition and the Salem Witch Trials).
- "Canals on Mars carry water to the civilization there" (see astronomer Schiaparelli).
- "The Hale-Bopp comet has arrived. We need to kill ourselves

so we can ride it to heaven" (see Heaven's Gate cult).

- "My Infinite is better than your Infinite, and I can do away with you if you believe otherwise" (see the Crusades).
- "There are plenty of bison; let's kill as many as we want" (see Buffalo Bill).
- "These beings (Africans, Chinese, Hutus, Armenians, Jews) aren't people, so they can be worked to death or killed" (see genocide and slavery).

Such concepts seemingly go on forever. Interestingly, the people who held these concepts considered them to be valuable and logical at the time. Furthermore, many people agreed with these speculations, despite the lack of verifiable evidence. I wonder what erroneous views you and I currently embrace because of this kind of speculative thinking!

4. THOUGHT STREAMS ARE ALWAYS ABOUT "ME"

Virtually all thought streams are focused on *ourselves*. We may have thought streaming about the opinions of others; whether a new song is good or not; how teachers, parents, or vehicles behave, or a variety of other topics. What these all have in common is "me."

That's right: Every thought stream focuses on our own selfish interests. We consider the opinions and the behavior of others or the qualities of new songs in relation to ourselves: *"How do I like them? How do they affect me? How can I change the way things are going?"* It's all about "me." What happens to others in this?

Even our thoughts about volunteering to help others concern "me," as in *"What will people think of my volunteering?"* With most thought streams selfishly focused on our own needs, how can we serve the interests of others? I trust you'll agree that it's good to care about others and consider their interests as we weigh the consequences of our own actions. But how can we do this in a balanced way? Only in the absence of thought streaming can we truly share what we have and what we do, receiving from others as well as taking part in a mutually beneficial give and take.

One of the more persuasive arguments for giving up the practice of thought streaming is that our goodwill and consideration for others can then naturally manifest. We can transform thoughts now aimed exclusively at us to include the interests of others. Don't you want others to consider you? Why not do the same for them?

In the selfishness of thought streaming, we also become dependent upon psychological defenses. Because virtually all thoughts are either directly or indirectly related to "me," we need to realistically face and deal with all the ugly thoughts and behaviors that we generate. For instance, some sexual predators rationalize their behavior by thought streaming about the supposed kindness of their sexual actions with children. Clearly, they haven't learned to deal with their thought streaming realistically.

Substance-dependent people with a family or a job deny their addiction to alcohol and drugs through thought streams about being functional in society. Embezzlers intellectually excuse their illegal financial moves through thought streams that validate their surreptitious skill: *"I've worked my butt off for this company, and what do I get? A measly bonus at the end of the year."* Physical abusers engage in thought streams in which they project their anger on to others, thereby justifying the bodily damage they do: *"He asked for it. That worm had it coming. If I don't stop him, who will?"* In all these examples, when we accept the contents of our thought streaming as factual, we don't deal with the world realistically.

What's harmful about selfish thought streaming—and it's all

selfish—is that we can inappropriately justify every wrongful action. Thought streaming offers our psychological defenses a variety of possible scenarios, and the ego chooses certain ones to make the actions seem right even though they're definitely not. We base every justification that we use on defensive thought streaming that originates from a harmful action we performed but don't want to recognize.

If there is "evil" in the world, I define it as the actions stemming from an excessively important "me" that severely minimizes the importance of others. Tyrants of the past and their accomplices committed acts without consideration for others. For example, those willing to steal, lie, and kill to get their way caused every genocide the world has experienced. On a less dramatic level, ordinary people hoard food, expropriate property, and defame others to gain recognition for themselves. Although the scale of harm varies from tyrants to "normal" people, their evil actions stem from an exaggerated sense of self-importance.

Therefore, I say, Be brave. Stop the thought streaming that supports an inordinately important "me." Recognize each harmful action you make, apologize, vow to cut off thought streaming, and move on with your life. Don't thought stream about the harm you caused, either; it's over so move on. You'll then live with courage and openness in this world.

5. THE FRUSTRATION CAUSED BY NOT GETTING ANSWERS

In the course of your life, you may have believed that thought streaming provided answers to questions. Perhaps you entertained thought streams about whether or not you should uproot the family to take a new job in a different city. You may have ruminated about the best ways to discipline your children, approach your boss on a difficult issue, or talk your spouse into viewing the world your way.

Ask yourself whether those thought streams ever helped you obtain an answer. Then ask yourself whether incessant thoughts occupied your mind too much and caused you sleeplessness, anxiety, a lack of intimacy with others, or an inability to pay attention to the life going on around you.

I would wager that you did not and do not find answers to your problems or questions through thought streaming. Essentially, you end up ruminating, becoming trapped in the primary error about thought streaming (the mistaken belief that because it seems similar to logical thinking, it solves problems). When you believe that logic can solve the long-standing discussion with your spouse about whether or not you should have children, the argument keeps going round and round in your head as you examine the benefits and potential problems from all angles. You might think like this: *"Children cost a lot of money to raise. They're a blessing when they grow into mature adults with whom you can become friends. But on the way, they'll break legs, need surgery, and fall out of love. What a painful mess we bring kids into. And what about the awful pain of childbirth!"*

However much you generate thought streams, the solution won't come through a point-by-point review followed by logical analysis, will it? It certainly won't! Both the actual discussion with your spouse and the mental monologue in your mind will leave you frustrated. When we try hard and can't find a solution to a vexing problem, it leaves us frustrated. The harder we try and the more thoughts we generate, the more frustrated we become.

6. A Negative Focus to Thought Content

Thought streaming becomes especially problematic when its content has a special, typically negative focus. First of all, thought streaming itself creates a problem. As I've mentioned, every stream of thoughts clouds our consciousness with mental noise that decreases our capacity to think clearly and have an open mind. When you consider the second problem—intense thought content that is sad, angry, suspicious, or escapist—clearly, thought streaming makes all situations worse.

When we direct our mental focus to these negative places, breaking off from them becomes even more difficult than usual because of the strong emotional charge. (Remember, all thought streams with a strong emotional charge are especially hard to stop.) Therefore, the individual who encourages thought streaming and whose mental content includes grief, anger, fear, control, greed or lack, suspicion, worthlessness, or vengefulness (and isn't that all of us at one time or another?) tends to be driven further and further into these negative states.

For example, people with tendencies toward sadness have trouble breaking out of despairing thoughts. Over long periods of time, their continuing sad thoughts turn into sad behavior patterns and perhaps even into depression. Likewise, people with a tendency towards fear may have difficulty breaking free of these thoughts. The world is filled with germs, which help us digest our food but which also cause us to become ill. If we allow our fearful thoughts to focus on germs, we can start over-washing our hands, over-cleaning our house, using a tissue or paper towel when we turn a door knob, and avoid handling money or being near people.

As another example, the approach of the high school prom often sends adolescents into negatively focused thought streaming. A young man might generate thought streams like the following: *"Even if I ask Linda, she'll turn me down. I bet Eva would go with me. Although I like Tiffany the most, I don't want to let her know yet, just in case she already has a boyfriend I don't know about. What a mess. Why do high schools even have prom nights anyway?"* As prom night draws near, many boys narrow their mental focus to asking out a girl and dealing with the fear of being rejected. Soon nothing else creeps into consciousness.

People who thought stream about revenge often find it becoming the primary driver of their lives. Nothing but vengeful thoughts run through their minds. Such a person might think, *"I'm sure he's responsible for my business going bankrupt. He had control of the finances. It was sneaky how he hid them from me. My life is totally ruined. I lost the business and all of the savings I poured into it. I've got to get Ralph back for that."*

As a revenge-seeking person dwells on his grievances, his mind continues to narrow its focus to the initial hurt he felt and the possible motives of the offending person. He thinks obsessively about how the person is an enemy of his and *only* an enemy, not a person with any positive traits. To end these compelling ruminations, the person must break out of the cycle of thought streaming. When it stops, so, too, does the accompanying emotional state. If it is not stopped, unpleasant results may follow.

The Hatfield and McCoy family feud is a good example of thought streaming obsessively focused on vengefulness. The feud spun out of control and into murderous activity in two families in a small rural area of the United States. A few years ago, the potential assassin, John Hinckley, also became obsessively focused through intense thought streaming, but in this case on becoming famous. Believing a need existed to please actress Jody Foster and gain her favor, Hinckley schemed misguidedly to win fame through an attempt on President's Reagan's life. However, don't fool yourself into believing that he was an especially malevolent person. The inability to control thought streaming causes most of our psychological problems. Hinckley just let it get too far out of control.

7. SOLIDIFYING CONCEPTS AND PREFERENCES

We shouldn't overestimate the harmful effect of solidifying concepts and preferences caused by thought streaming because the world is grayer than our typical wish for black and white categories. Indeed, we often have to cope with issues that aren't as distinct as our minds would like them to be. Even the apparently clear cases of yes/no and right/wrong pose major difficulties that we must recognize as being part of how things are.

Unfortunately, thought streaming narrows down our perspective along with our focus. In doing so, it rapidly solidifies the world into more rigid constructs than actually exist. At face value, this tendency appears helpful, but it actually imposes onto our worldview a distorted, oversimplified sense of reality.

As an example, let's look at gender, a seemingly clear cut category that really isn't. What is gender, anyway? What part of gender categorization is based on anatomy, and is anatomy all there is to understanding gender? If it is, why don't we just use the word "anatomy"? What part of gender is based on chromosomes? What part is based on behavior such as sexual preference? Hormones also play an important role in gender. Part of the bias against gay, lesbian, intersex, and transgender individuals stems not from their behavior, as many believe, but from our own sense of insecurity. Our language tells us that gender is a distinct category, yet by example people who are gay, lesbian, and intersex tell us otherwise. We can't put them into our neatly defined categories but want to keep clear boundaries on our classifications. We seem to use categories that are too rigidly fortified to describe the realities of the world.

Language has forced on the human race the creation of categories where none naturally exists. Because we believe these classifications help us, we've developed the problem of trying to make the world fit our language. Since this just can't be done, it only adds to our frustration.

Consider, also, the example of race, which appears to be a relatively clear-cut category. But here again the same problem of forced categories exists. In the United States we use relatively few categories, while before 1990 the Republic of South Africa had more numerous classifications.

Geneticists tell us there is more difference within "racial groups" of the same skin color than between groups of people with different skin colors. As with gender, we simply can't make artificial racial categorizations in a meaningful way, a condition that might frustrate some people. Often we try to make the world more understandable by an overreliance on categories, but this process has limited benefits. When we classify complex individuals in simplified categories, we exclude qualified people from educational and career opportunities. This happens because thought streaming, the real origin of categories, relies on repetition, categorization, and exclusion. Through these activities, thought streaming solidifies concepts and distorts the world. When we stop our tendency to thought stream, the boundaries supporting these categories lessen appropriately, and a truer picture of reality comes into clearer view.

Recently, I had the opportunity to sit in front of a picture that had numerous small black dots on a light-colored background. My mind ran on and on, creatively pulling together sets of dots and mentally organizing them into faces. Perhaps you've had a similar experience. I saw old women, jokers, and odd-shaped people with craggy faces. In reality, there were no faces in that picture at all.

Furthermore, the artist didn't intend to have people see faces in the artwork. Because the mind tends to organize the world into categories, it makes faces from dots, specific racial groups from a continuum of human appearances, and two gender categories from a continuum of sexual orientations. If we realize this tendency, we won't let our mind run away carelessly and believe unquestionably all that it tells us.

When we inappropriately solidify concepts and preferences, we harm ourselves by believing more in our categories than in reality. The Southern California wildfires of 2003 showed this in a geopolitical sense. The wildfires burned land and structures. Officials, however, categorized the land into parcels according to local, state, federal, and Indian lands. The fires knew none of these categorizations. Much frustration and damage resulted when federal firefighting resources couldn't be used on state lands.

Thinking Outside the "Box"

Finally, in this arena of over-conceptualization, business people value "thinking outside the box." They want to see issues more clearly and come up with novel solutions in order to deliver better goods and services and make more money. The "box" that we want to think outside of represents our commonly held but inappropriately solidified conceptions. For example, one large company that viewed itself only as a computer maker has now expanded to offer personnel services. This company "broke the mold" and reconceptualized its work areas far beyond its original scope of activity.

Thinking outside the conceptual box has altered other businesses, too. Worksites themselves are changing. Previously, white-collar employees showed up at their desk in the office wearing a suit. Now many white-collar employees work from home and dress in a bathrobe as they handle teleconferencing calls. Stores that have typically sold small-to-medium-sized goods (like gift cards, novelties, and tourist items) have transformed themselves by adding parcel shipping services to their businesses as another way to make money. Traditional retail stores are now blurring the lines between offering goods and services. What is a store anyway? Whereas we previously defined a store as a retail shop on Main Street, many businesses have broken even that mold. Now "virtual" stores exist whose main address is simply a website on the Internet.

We know that categories can and do interfere with our understanding of a problem, but we use them anyway. They usually offer quick, convenient ways to understand an issue. Once conceptualized, however, they're hard to deconstruct because thought streaming maintains the shaping process that fixed them in the first place.

If we want to think "outside the box" (and I agree with others who say we should), we need to break down artificial categorizations so we can grasp the truth of a situation. When we stop thought streaming, we end the process of maintaining "the box" in a fixed conceptualization. We then have a chance to look at any and every issue anew.

PUTTING OURSELF IN THE "BOX"

The most destructive "box" is the one in which we place our own selves. Too often, we use our past experiences as containers to describe who we are today. We tell ourselves, *"Once a householder, always a householder. My worthiness depends on what I own. Who I am is fully determined by my past."* We too easily can place ourselves, as well as others, into common categories that restrict our ability to live flexibly in this world.

We categorize ourselves and others as rational or emotional, Republican or Democrat, pro-life or pro-choice, a true believer or non-believer, intelligent or dumb. Yet are these categorizations completely true of us or others? Certainly not. We may have some of these characteristics, but no category ever defines us completely. At times, we may feel more like a Republican, pro-choice, non-believer, while at other times we my feel more like a Democrat, pro-life, true-believer. At other times, we would never even define ourselves in these ways. We are, thankfully, more than these categories. Behind the screen of thoughts that categorize us into one box or another, we are more flexible than any of these restricting labels.

By getting through the screen of thought streaming and the categories it creates, we have the opportunity to see our basic, open, and infinitely flexible being that is a true joy to live from. Who are we? Are we what is currently housed within this container of skin we call a body? If so, who were we ten years ago when we held a similar view but looked through a different container of skin? Are we the sum total of our experiences? Are we the sum of our favorite experiences? Are we the consciousness that has the experiences? Are we the sense of aliveness or beingness that is behind this curtain of thought streams? Just what are our limits?

On her 90th birthday, I asked my grandmother what it felt like being that old. She said it felt as if she was still 16 but she couldn't walk around as easily. I believe she was saying that she identified more with her consciousness than with her body. Our consciousness doesn't seem to age; the consciousness with which we see the world today is the same consciousness that saw the world when we were younger.

However, we can't say the same for our body. Look at old pictures of yourself. Do you look the same today as you did at birth, at age 10, or at twenty years of age? Of course not. Yet something consistent and unchanging—consciousness—has seen and heard the world all these years. Typically, we often use our consciousness as a self-reference. We refer to "these legs of mine," "these arms of mine," and "this body of mine." We mean that these legs, arms, and body of "mine" are owned by the consciousness that animates us. Reflecting on this, how can we believe that consciousness, our fundamental self, has any limits? It doesn't, of course. We have complete freedom beyond anything we've learned from our parents and our society.

When we stop our thought streaming and connect with our fundamental self, we discover that we have a limitless capacity for change, understanding, and innovation. Unfortunately, all too often we waste this inherent freedom because of our strong conceptualizations. Given a chance, we all can play sports, run businesses, support people in need, be creative in a wide variety of artistic media, and live according to our fundamental joy. Thought streaming, however, keeps us imprisoned behind the walls of a "box". As thought streaming subsides, we free our minds, and the barriers to personal change can melt away.

NEUROSIS – RESISTANCE TO A FLEXIBLE SELF

We're subject to a diagnosis of neurosis when we harbor any rigid sense about ourselves. As a result, we may experience feelings of emptiness or worthlessness, prolonged sadness or anger, a need for controlling our life circumstances, or an inflated feeling of superiority. If, for example, I solidify my sense of self around the notion that I'm better and more competent than you, I won't allow my sense of self to be flexible enough to be better and more competent at times, and worse than you and less competent than you at others. The rigid stances we hold clearly cause problems, either for ourselves or others.

For example, those with a strong need to control things may inwardly feel out of control. Likewise, people who hold inappropriately high standards may feel sad, angry, empty, worthless, or inferior because they can't achieve the perfection they espouse. If they chronically maintain these artificial standards, the accompanying emotional states will cause them to live unhappily. Often people with these standards can't come to realistic terms with their own emotionality. Someone who has a need for control or who feels incapable, unloved, or blocked from achieving, may benefit from what I call Root Therapy."

In this approach, we accept the reality of a situation rather than living with an overly rigid sense of self (such as "I must always be in control.") This therapy, which is quite easy to undertake, consists of two parts. First, for 15 minutes, we practice noticing and stopping our thought streaming, which helps clear the mind of conceptualizations that hinder openness. Then, keeping the problem in mind, we simply keep asking ourself one question: *"And what's so bad about this?"* As we persist in our exploration, the question helps us repeatedly dive through layer after layer of the problem until we encounter the single-most, emotionally charged aspect at the core of the problem.

Let's use the example of someone with an overly strong need for control, Root Therapy would go like this: The person would sit quietly, noticing and stopping his thought streaming for 15 minutes; subsequently, he would ask himself, *"And what's so bad about being out of control?"* Answers to repeated self-questioning might go something like this: *"I would lose money. And what's so bad about this? I'd feel afraid. And what's so bad about this? I'd need to live on the street. And what's so bad about this? I wouldn't be able to take care of myself, so I'd die there alone."*

Through Root Therapy, this person has discovered that his strong need for control relates to a hidden fear of dying alone. We all must come to accept the reality that we will die and that circumstances may be out of our control. Once this fact has been brought to light, the person can then deal with his fear in a realistic way. As this example demonstrates, until we free our mind from solidified beliefs, such as the unrealistic desire to be in control at all times, neuroses will continue to plague our existence.

We can resolve our strong conceptualizations about ourselves when we examine and come to terms with the root problems we didn't wish to see. When we truly and deeply accept that we feel helpless, inferior, or angry in certain situations, we gain freedom from our neurotic defenses that express as our exaggerated need for self-esteem, the need to be right, and so forth. We then can begin to see who we truly are.

TRY THIS:

ON a planned and regular basis, look at your thought streams and actively attempt to stop every *easy* one you can. I suggest that every time you have your first cup of coffee or tea in the morning, use this time to notice your thought streaming and try to stop or distract yourself from becoming involved in each thought stream. Don't worry about the difficult ones. By practicing on the easier ones now, you will build the capability to work with those that are more difficult later. In addition, by stopping those you can right now, you will more fully enjoy the taste and smell of your coffee or tea!

CHAPTER NINE

The Practical Results of Giving Up Thought Streaming: 1

Psychology and Personal Relationships

"Worry gives a small thing a big shadow."
—Swedish Proverb

C O N S I D E R what your life would be like if thought streaming didn't take up as much energy as it does. As you know, uncontrolled thought streams play an ever-present role in your interior life. Thoughts stream along on every topic imaginable. Whatever the circumstances of your occupation, activities, or relationships, you'll surely experience improvements when you're better able to pay attention. When the screen of inattention raised by thought streaming is dropped completely, you'll inevitably improve your ability to concentrate completely on your activities.

In the next few chapters, I'll discuss the benefits of giving up thought streaming in our lives. I'll investigate some burdensome social and personal issues that face us, but these aren't the only areas affected by thought streaming. If you look to your own life, you'll easily identify certain circumstances that are strongly influenced by thought streaming. We must all work on these in our own way.

PSYCHOLOGY AND THOUGHT STREAMING

Psychiatry, psychotherapy, and clinical psychology do not typically concern themselves with thought streaming, nor do they work on decreasing it in hopes of generating increased insight and creativity. As I noted earlier, psychotherapists typically focus more on the content of thought rather than on the process of thought. I don't wish to oversimplify the field, but clinicians often concern themselves with a client's dreams, behavior patterns, specific thoughts generating specific emotions, and early childhood conditioning. In a psychotherapeutic session for an adult, therefore, the initial therapy often turns to an examination of childhood conditioning, how it manifests itself in the present day, and how the client might break free of it.

Psychotherapists have minimized the plain fact of thought streaming and its detrimental effects on people. As I've explained, thought streaming contributes to the suffering of people with anxiety, depression, low self-esteem, poor interpersonal relationships, inattention, and lack of concentration, as well as overall low quality of life. I won't delve deeply into these conditions, since much has already been written about them in the traditional psychological literature. I simply want to increase awareness about the damage we inadvertently do to ourselves because we don't hold our mind still with focused attention.

I believe the time is ripe for determining whether we should codify "thought streaming" as a category of clinical diagnosis. I see no benefit to thought streaming; I see only harm. As a problem, it transcends those of other diagnostic categories, such as anxiety and depression; in fact, these conditions actually manifest as subsets of uncontrolled thought streaming. To this end, I sent a letter to the American Psychological and American Psychiatric Associations describing the change I recommend (see the Appendix).

If thought streaming were accepted as an appropriate focus for psychotherapy, patients would benefit by experiencing a fundamental mental clarity as the harmful aspects of thought streaming dropped away. We need mental clarity as a basic necessity for healthy, happy living, yet few of us have it or strive for it. Because thought streaming obscures mental clarity, patients who are besieged by excessive thought can't hear what their psychotherapists say to them. Thought streaming blocks their mind and their ability to listen and receive help. If psychotherapists would first assess the extent of patients' thought streaming, they would know better how to help their clients in therapy.

If thought streaming were fast and uncontrolled, work on reducing its volume and intensity might be the first priority of psychotherapy. If understanding the nature of thought streaming were seen as an appropriate direction for treatment, patients would transform themselves by developing mental clarity and removing the harmful influence of runaway thought. Imagine for yourself how improvements in mental clarity would help your own life. Now imagine yourself in the midst of a personal struggle, say with a spouse, a child, or a co-worker. Do you see how having mental clarity would greatly assist you in handling the problem? For sure, it would!

ANXIETY AND DEPRESSION
As mental disorders, anxiety and depression share certain similarities, including a significant amount of rumination or internal monologue. In the future, we will increasingly see a relationship between these conditions and their genetic or biological predispositions. Perhaps brain chemicals or their receptors will be identified as a primary cause of these disorders. However, no top researchers believe that

the full effects of anxiety and depression are exclusively genetic in origin.

Much of the management of these problems is in our own hands. Clearly, we can help ourselves overcome anxiety and depression by controlling our thought streaming tendencies. When we suffer from these disorders, we engage in an internal monologue that focuses attention on feelings of fear, sadness, or worthlessness; often we feel incapable of meeting the world's demands.

While many of us have sad or anxious thoughts at times, they don't disturb us day in and day out. By becoming more skilled in not entering into these kinds of thought streams, or at least mentally turning away from those that support a sense of fear, sadness, or worthlessness, we can help alleviate a downward spiral into these disorders.

The following two examples are of people who did not practice stopping thought streaming. Instead, they became caught up in obsessive thoughts, giving their thought streams credence as if they either contained useful information or could help them solve their problems. Of course, we know this to be an invalid response because thought streaming is harmful, not helpful.

THOUGHT STREAMING ON A PAST TRAUMA

A client of mine, James, had severe symptoms of post-traumatic stress disorder (PTSD), a combination of anxiety and depression stemming from a particularly damaging or troubling event that happened during the Vietnam War. James was standing with two other soldiers when one was shot from a great distance and killed, probably by a sniper. Although James had seen others die around him, this specific incident escalated into a trauma by sending him into a strong thought streaming mode.

His thought streams revolved around trying to understand why another soldier had been killed and not him. Because James wanted to survive, he tried figuring it out. Unfortunately, he still believed the primary error about thought streaming (that it's similar to thinking and can help us solve our problems).

At the time of the killing, he had been smoking and "kicking back," as the other fellow had been. "We all looked the same in our fatigues" he said, "and we were standing side by side when it happened." James was dressed the same as his buddy, and many other facts seemed just as similar. Based on the commonality of these points, his thoughts took off relentlessly, and he thought up one scenario after another to explain why his friend was killed and he was still alive.

James' life became focused on coming up with a myriad of possible scenarios to help him understand why the sniper didn't kill him. As we talked about this problem, he said things like, "Why wasn't it me? Why am I alive and not him? He had kids and I didn't, so I should have died." No answer ever appeased him. He felt out of control and guilt-ridden for having survived this situation. Fourteen years later, James was still having thought streams about this event.

He would have been far better not encouraging those thoughts. What good did they serve? He couldn't voluntarily release these thoughts; instead, they captured and tormented him for years. If he had learned to stop his thought streaming, his life would have moved in a more positive direction. During my few weeks of therapy with him, James couldn't see the plain fact that his thoughts were the problem. He couldn't resolve the primary error about thought streaming and, unfortunately, his life continued to be seriously impaired because of this lack of insight. He was more fascinated by the question of "why" he didn't die and by his survivor guilt than he was interested in seeing that his problems stemmed from thought streaming and that he could resolve them by the practice of stopping his thought streams.

THOUGHT STREAMING ON FEAR

A woman I know named Ann is plagued by an unnaturally strong fear of going outside her home. She has a diagnosable condition termed *agoraphobia*. Her fears don't come from the neighborhood, as hers is a friendly one. She has no significant health problems, nor is she excessively cautious in other areas of her life. Yet her fear persists.

I believe that Ann's uncontrolled thoughts contribute to her problem. She has consistent and recurring thought streams about a possible future injury, even though no actual threats to her body exist. She chooses to have thought streams about becoming injured, about how serious those injuries would be, and about the treatments she would then require. For example, Ann often says, "I'm worried about being hit by a car" or "I'm concerned about being bitten by the neighbor's dog; he seems so mean."

When I ask Ann about her thought streaming, however, she says, "It's very limited. I don't stream on with my thoughts very much." I find this hard to believe, since she remains extremely fearful of going outside her home, and she continually expresses fears about cars and animals. Ann's thought streaming has become so familiar to her that she recognizes only new thoughts and thought streaming topics (those not related to her constant fear) as forms of thought streaming. In other words, she's become so accustomed to her fearful thought streaming that it seems normal to her.

Like Ann, many of us believe our thought streaming is normal and valid. Thought streaming may pervade our consciousness to such an extent that it escapes our notice. As an antidote, I recommend the continual practice of noticing thought streaming and disentangling from it as soon as possible.

SOCIAL PHOBIAS AND THE FEAR OF PUBLIC SPEAKING

Many people feel uneasy when meeting new people or when called upon to speak in front of an audience. Such anxieties are so widespread that support groups such as Toastmasters exist. Psychologists have done extensive research to determine why people feel this way and how they can best overcome this apparent disability. In fact, because interest in this area is so strong, pharmaceutical companies have been studying antidepressants to see whether they can help ameliorate the condition.

For many conditions, including "social anxiety," I have difficulty accepting a traditional psychological view, with its diagnosis and strategy for treatment. I view social anxiety as a manifestation of how our thought processes negatively influences our lives, a view that mainstream psychology and psychiatry minimize.

Behaviorally oriented therapists tend to believe that the socially anxious person is conditioned as a youngster to be fearful of others. Cognitively focused psychologists are interested in how specific thoughts support specific emotions and behaviors. Genetically oriented professionals may cite a hyperactive adrenocortical system as the cause of too many excitatory hormones or neurotransmitters circulating in the body. Other professionals may postulate that the audience represents a stern father figure and that the "child" in the speaker therefore responds anxiously.

These are all interesting plausibilities, but I think the cause of anxiety is simply uncontrolled thought streams. When we thought stream, we inappropriately solidify facts into concepts and representations. A person who fears public speaking conceptualizes himself or herself into a "box," which may relate to a personal insecurity about shyness, a perceived lack of intelligence, or a perceived physical unattractiveness. If you talk to someone who is nervous about speaking, you will hear thought streams like the following: *"I hope I don't look like a dope out there. I feel unprepared, so I probably will look like an idiot. I wish I had a better suit because I might look like I know something. Others seem to do this well, but I'm just bad at presentations. Why shouldn't I be nervous? I really don't like to have a lot of people around."*

In any case, the speaker has inadvertently formulated a strong opinion about his capability and has also formulated a belief about the capability of the audience. When the speaker believes his capability is less than that of the audience, the thought streaming itself starts to examine the content of the situation and become the cause of anxiety.

When the speaker's unconscious and false identity establishes that he is less intelligent or less attractive than others, the thoughts streaming through consciousness carry this new content: *"I'm a bad speaker. I'm boring, and I really don't know what I'm talking about."* Thoughts about low intelligence or unattractiveness may intrude into consciousness at an increasing pace, along with others about clothing, hairstyle, makeup, or perfume, which are concerns about physical attractiveness in a different guise.

If the speaker finds himself in the false "box" about inferior intelligence, his thought streaming might look like this: *"My handouts aren't so good. I wish I had looked at my slides before the presentation because I don't feel they're in the right order. My talk doesn't relate to the topic I was supposed to speak about. I don't believe I really have much to talk about that could make a difference in people's lives."*

These thought streams are not only unnecessary, but ultimately harmful. For our hapless speaker, the solidified sense of stupidity he experiences plus intense thought streaming on the topic of intelligence or attractiveness means that anxiety must surely build and so adversely affect his speaking performance.

Without thought streaming, the speaker's conceptualized representation of himself will be far less solidified; hence, he will have reduced anxiety. The speaker will not berate himself with self-abusive monologues. Internally driven thought streams will no longer cause anxiety. Isn't it pleasant to hear a speaker who talks openly, with no sign of undue self-consciousness, and who gives undivided attention both to the audience and the topic? Only speakers who have defeated their thought streaming tendencies can accomplish this.

THE NERVOUS BREAKDOWN

A "nervous breakdown," as it's known in the popular media, is not a formal term used by psychotherapists. Yet it remains a useful description for a person in circumstances of overwhelming mental or emotional stress. From my vantage point, a nervous breakdown is a condition of exhaustion directly related to, and perhaps even caused by, thought streaming that has increased past the psychological limits that a person can endure.

People who have gone through nervous breakdowns report having intense and incessant thoughts about their fears, careers, perceived failings, and desires for increased status. Their thought streams might resemble the following: "I was well-respected. I had a loving family and oversaw a large budget at work. Look at me now. No one respects me. I let my physical appearance decline dramatically. I don't get invited anywhere. My family doesn't call, either." If we listen carefully to what people in this condition say, we find that it's actually their thought streaming that's spiraled out of control. Since they can't constrain the speed or intensity of their thought streams, their personal capacity reaches overload. As a result, they have to be physically removed from their life circumstances, typically by hospitalization, to break the hold of this aggressive form of thought streaming.

I suspect that any form of sadness or anxiety can turn into a "nervous breakdown." The emotional strain might have any specific source—health, personal relationships, career, or the achievement of goals. Whether we have a nervous breakdown may depend on whether we control our thought streaming or whether it controls us.

PERSONAL RELATIONSHIPS

We humans are social animals. Among all our relationships, we most highly prize the close, personal ones. They give us some of our greatest pleasure, as well as some of our deepest pain. We never forget the happiness of our early childhood friendships. Nor do we forget the pain of being betrayed by someone we thought was our friend.

Our thoughts and emotions greatly influence our personal relationships, so much so that often our opinion of someone doesn't jive with reality. Do you remember your first crush, the object of your affection who could do no wrong? Do you remember when you fell out of love with that person? Did you ever like your boss and then have a mutual falling out of favor? Did you and a partner ever get along well with another couple and then have irreconcilable differences? In all these instances, did reality change, or was there interference from thought streaming?

Let's explore two main points about personal relationships. First, we prejudge many relationships before we even enter into them. This prejudice causes us to score the relationship's potential for success before many of the truly important facts are known. We prejudge because we have natural as well as stereotypical preferences for others, based on factors such as physical health, overall appearance, and psychological attitude. Because she is an attractive woman, we may feel an affinity with her before we discover her self-centeredness. A new religious leader at our place of worship may lack verbal skills in delivering speeches, yet his ability to serve the group may encourage others to follow his example. We all have preferences, but experience teaches us that it's best if we hold them lightly. We might be surprised about what we learn.

Secondly, thought streaming reinforces our prejudice and preferences, solidifying them with its own form of repetition and quasi-logic. In the example of the new religious leader, we may judge him inept because he seems inarticulate. In response to him, we might think: *"Wow, did you hear what he said to Jake when they were standing at the casket? I can't believe he was so brutally honest, talking about the death of his child. Where does he come off talking like that? I wonder if he missed the etiquette class in seminary."*

As we have seen, thought streams like this can go on and on. They encourage and solidify our belief that the religious leader is inept. They also convince us that besides being inarticulate, he is generally uncaring, unfeeling, and even stupid. Yet this stereotyping simply results from the tendency of thought streaming to solidify or overly conceptualize the world. Our incessant and repetitive mental monologue convinces us of some truth, even though we have only a few facts. From one overheard comment at a casket, we have stereotyped our beloved religious leader into an uncaring and stupid moron! It certainly isn't a fair appraisal of his worth, yet the work of thought streaming has done its damage. If we do not entertain thought streaming, we let more information come to us, suspend the judgments involved in stereotyping, and make truer assessments of people and the world around us.

Thought streaming on relationship issues can have immensely negative effects in our lives. When we learn to stop thought streaming, we will:

1. Stop dwelling on fights of the past.
2. Approach each new relationship with freshness so we can judge each on its own merits.
3. Support communication by letting us hear what the other has to say without being distracted by a noisy mind.

Imagine a close personal relationship with someone you love. If you or your loved one is stuck in thought streaming about love or anger, the distance between you increases. Let's say that your thought streams rolled on like this: *"I really like this person. I hope she brings me all the joy I deserve. If she brings me this joy, I'll do so much for her that she can't imagine. We'll treat each other as king and queen."* As you can see, this man is brushing aside the reality of daily life and replacing it with a fantasy life as king and queen that actually distances him from his lover. Similarly, thought streams based on another topic, such as anger, would also distance him from his beloved.

When one or both partners stop thought streaming, intimacy increases. Without preconceptions about how the other should behave, look, or feel, partners can experience each other more directly. We can exchange views, hopes, and memories completely without fear of derision from the other. Now open communication exists and supports the partnership. Thought streaming that is under control doesn't interfere with current problems, nor does it bring negative memories or concerns about the future inappropriately into the day-to-day struggles we all have. How pleasant life is without thought streaming. How warm the intimacy!

THE FLEXIBILITY OF THE PERSONALITY

I'll give an example from my own life of how thought streaming relates to flexibility of the personality. As a supervisor at work, I was overseeing a woman who wanted to be a better mentor to others. Susan was a fine person with great potential. However, she became stuck in a relationship role that was rather rigid. Susan related to her staff as a superior, rather than as someone who simply had more experience and training. She told her staff what to do and didn't allow others to express their opinions about her requests. For example, Susan might tell her staff to make a set of telephone calls to subcontractors about specific budget items and not tell her staff the reasoning behind these calls. Her thought streaming went along the lines of *"I'm the boss, and these people should just do what I say."* This approach, which was producing relationships based on a hierarchy of superiors and inferiors, didn't accord with either the company culture or how she wanted to be viewed by her staff.

To remedy the situation, I asked Susan to take an on-line test related to personality style. Then I had her take the test again, with the intention of mentally adjusting her rigid supervisory style to that of a cooperative staff counselor. I told her, "Please think about your staff as people who were your classmates at college, and you all have the job of helping in a fundraising event." When she had settled into thought streaming that placed her back at college with friends, she took the test again. The test results showed that she had the flexibility to adopt either style: She could be a cooperative counselor or a controlling supervisor. By encouraging her to change her thought streaming content, I saw the depth of her relationships with her staff increase, and Susan became a more effective mentor.

We also talked about the problems that thought streaming itself produced. In some circumstances, being a cooperative counselor was as counterproductive as being a rigid supervisor. Sometimes Susan would have to step outside the "box" of counselor and supervisor to handle a problem in an unforeseen way. In such situations, dropping thought streaming helps us step beyond exclusive identification with any personality style. The mental clarity and openness that a lack of thought streaming provides enhances our ability to adapt to the world of ever-changing circumstances.

Self-Esteem, Self-Worth, and Anger

When we entertain a great volume of thought streams, we create trouble for ourselves. We all have successes and failures in life, in greater or lesser degrees. If we need to acknowledge, for example, that we've failed at some task, it's best to simply accept the failure as a fact and move on with our life. Often, however, we trigger thought streams like the following: *"I'm so stupid to believe I could have gotten that job"* or *"I can never get anyone interested in me romantically"* or *"My friends never want to do what I want to do."* These examples show how dramatic we can be in reacting to small failures. A new success might soon come along, as long as we don't overburden ourselves with unreasonable expectations of achievement. If we allow the negative thought streaming to continue unchecked, it will adversely influence our outlook.

Repeated thought streams of apparent failure, incompetence, or self-disparagement can exaggerate plain and simple facts. Year in and year out, thought streams of failure can weaken our mental outlook. Self-esteem, the day-to-day sense of personal value, can suffer without just cause. *"Boy, I really did that job poorly"* might start a long, self-incriminating thought stream. As it continues, our self-worth, the longer-term sense of our personal value, can suffer as well. We might think, *"I didn't get my timesheet project done on time. Mary didn't want to go to the movies with me because she thinks I'm a loser. I can't even train my new dog to sit up."* Such thought streams skew our view of ourselves and how the world perceives us. Because of consistent self-demeaning thoughts, the value of our life soon diminishes. We can develop an emotional response of self-loathing or anger that can be maintained for years by streams of thought. Thus it's better not to enter into thought streams at all; the next best thing is to stop them from recurring just as quickly as you can.

A CASE STUDY IN THOUGHT STREAMS OF DEPRESSION

A client of mine, Joan, was depressed. She was mentally focused on how far her life had fallen socially and financially since her husband had died. As a child, Joan had been part of a family that was financially well off. They had a beautiful house, and the children were well cared for. In her twenties, she fell in love with a man "beneath her station" who was smart, charming, and loving. They raised one child into late adolescence before her husband died.

With little savings, Joan had to go to work. All she knew was sewing, so she became a seamstress at a local clothing factory. But this work didn't accord with her expectations of how her life should unfold. Feeling unprepared and ill-equipped to support herself and her son, she developed a false self-concept of worthlessness. Although her needs were modest and she made enough money to pay the bills, she still felt worthless. Joan believed she had too little skill to overcome the financial fall that followed her husband's death.

Her thought streams of worthlessness, which caused her unremitting grief, led to three suicide attempts. Her thoughts were incessantly distressing: *"I was so stupid to fall in love with Joe. My parents were right; a successful marriage depends more on money than on love. I never wanted to work, and look what I'm doing now. My apartment is terrible; how can I move from there when I don't have any money? My parents were right after all."* Joan remained continually lost in thought about her marriage, her husband's death, and her seemingly bleak financial status. If she could have separated herself from her thought streaming, she would have seen all the trouble it was causing her.

Fortunately, Joan's story has a happy ending. She had some successes that made her reevaluate her false sense of worthlessness. She got a modest promotion at work, and her son moved nearby and offered her emotional support. Seeing these changes as small measures of worthiness, Joan began to question her habitual sense of worthlessness. With encouragement to look into the validity of her thought streams, she started the process of resolving the primary error of thought streaming.

Most of us don't take the time to examine our thoughts; it never even occurs to us that we should. When we finally do it, we're on the road to a happier mental life. To be sure, thought streams of sadness and depression are difficult to overcome, yet it's well worth a try. However, we don't have to tackle the more difficult problems first. We can all extract ourselves from a few negative thought streams, and we certainly can remove ourselves from thought streams on trivial matters.

So there's a start. We begin by extricating ourselves from as many thought streams as possible while holding the intention to keep from getting into as many others as we can. That's all any of us can do. With this start, we can begin a practice that leads to better mental health, and, step by step, we inevitably find our way to greater peace of mind.

FREE YOUR MIND

CHAPTER TEN

The Practical Results of Giving Up Thought Streaming: 2

Health, Sports, Business and Education

"After a good system for putting is adopted, all the rest is mental."
—Paraphrasing Harvey Penick, golf coach

HEALTH-RELATED QUALITY OF LIFE

Let's continue with our exploration of the practical benefits that accrue when we give up thought streaming. We'll begin by looking at the health industry. Health plans, health insurers, government agencies, and pharmaceutical companies use a term called "the health-related quality of life" (HRQOL) to measure the extent to which we're satisfied with the quality of our health. These groups have an interest in determining our levels of satisfaction and health. They seek improvements in the health of the population while trying to maintain the lowest possible costs of individual care.

If they keep health care costs low, the reasoning goes, the benefits may be spread across more of the public. Health professionals use standard assessment methods that include scores of social, physical, vocational, and psychological functioning, as well as the level of pain in an individual's life to determine an overall level of health-related quality of life. Yet these companies and agencies have overlooked the impact of thought streaming in assessing quality of life. It's time to add this factor into the mix so that we can distinguish people's perceptions of their health from the facts of their health conditions.

Some Feel Satisfied Even in a State of Disability

While health-related quality of life is important to us all, it has remarkable variability among people. To this point, I had a discussion with a leading academic researcher who assesses HRQOL. We were talking about data he had gathered that showed some unusual responses. He had new information indicating that about 10 percent of people with end-stage renal disease (ESRD) who needed dialysis to live reported relatively high levels of HRQOL. From his point of view, this seemed unreasonable, given that people with a diagnosis of ESRD have a dramatically shortened life span. In addition, they had limited life activities because they had to spend a few hours every other day getting dialysis at a local clinic. If they missed a dialysis appointment, their bodies quickly became ill with uremia, a form of blood poisoning. Many people besides this researcher would find it hard to believe that these patients reported high levels of HRQOL. However, I think I know why.

Misery from the Disease Itself Plus Thought Streams about the Disease

The relationship between thought streaming and HRQOL is an important one—more important than most people realize. Principally, the relationship concerns the unnecessary suffering that we add through thought streaming to the fundamental pain of our illness. We would be better off without this additional mental anguish. Isn't the illness itself bad enough?

Patients with ESRD certainly know that their health is seriously compromised; that's the plain truth of the situation. I believe that the small percentage of patients who report a high life quality have found a way to cut off their thought streams and live realistically with their immediate experience. Instead of encouraging thought streams about their future state of health, they most likely have figured out how to stop this type of thought streaming. They don't indulge this kind of thought stream: *"Why did this happen to me? I hate being hooked up to that dialysis machine. Hey, those needles hurt! If I can't get a kidney transplant, I just don't know what I'll do. Our money is running low, and yet I still can't work at my old job."* Life without this thought streaming is simpler, more joyous, and mentally easier. Does a negative thought stream help someone with ESRD. No. Can this kind of thought streaming be stopped? Yes, it can.

None of us knows what our future health will be. Why, then, should we entertain dramatic thoughts of infirmities not yet felt? No one knows how quickly an illness we have will cause our functioning to deteriorate. So why encourage thoughts of a rapid decline? Apparently, those 10 percent of ESRD patients who are enjoying life have found ways to keep from obsessing about their apparent poor health. They lead a much happier existence than those who have not adopted such practices.

ESRD is a serious problem, but not many people have this illness. More commonly, we have problems such as heart disease, diabetes, stroke, obesity, and cancer. Have you noticed that some people seem overwhelmingly concerned when diagnosed with one of these illnesses, while others are less dramatically affected? Perhaps you have seen this in yourself. In my case, I get more emotionally concerned when I get a respiratory problem, such as bronchitis or a chest cold, than when I have other illnesses. My thoughts want to stream on about the possibility of suffocating. Yes, it's overly dramatic to equate suffocating with a chest cold, but that's what happens to me. Thankfully, I know about the harmfulness of thought streaming and don't travel down that road of mental anguish anymore. But many people do. I was once at the hospital bedside of a friend who was diagnosed with early-stage prostate cancer. Basically, he was lost in thought about his impending death, even though it was pure conjecture and worry on his part. His thought streams surged like this: *"What will my kids do without me? I won't get to play ball with my son. My wife and kids will have a tough time without me. I hope my mom doesn't take this too badly."*

On a more trivial level of illness, people with hypochondriasis magnify even their most modest illnesses. Would you suppose that thought streaming might have something to do with this? Our thoughts can run amok for any reason and at any time. Example: *"This cut I got while working on the oily engine looks red, like it's infected. I saw an infection on television, some kind of flesh-eating bacteria. It took that guy's arm off in less than a week!"* Why shouldn't our thoughts run amok when we're ill? They can but it's just adding unnecessary suffering to the basic pain or problem. We have a choice, and I hope more of us take it.

Sports and Thought Streaming

I consider the most challenging aspect of sports to be maintaining focus and attention. Of course, those who participate in sports need to be physically fit. To *excel* in sports, however, they must also develop the mental aspect of the game to a high level.

Sports magazines and sports psychology publications abound in articles about the mental aspect of sports. They unanimously indicate that enhanced attention and concentration are the hallmarks of athletic excellence. I hope that professional coaches and other sports enthusiasts will take my ideas about thought streaming seriously and apply them in a disciplined way to enhance athletic performance.

At the Highest Levels, the Challenge Is Mental

Some of our top athletes suffer from the fear of failing in public. They may believe that the task at hand is too great a challenge, or they may feel too shy to perform in a large auditorium filled with people. While there are many psychological challenges in sports, athletes must overcome them all to reach the championship level. We've all seen competitors who display failures of will in sports and games: gymnasts who run off the floor in the midst of their routine, golfers who suddenly drop from leadership positions on the course, and chess players who tumble in their standings. In these cases, thought streaming sabotaged personal performance.

These examples of thought streaming gone awry in sports lead naturally to the questions, "Why do we enjoy sports and recreation? Just what are we recreating from?" In an earlier chapter I mentioned that we seek sports and recreation to get back in touch with our original aliveness, our original sense of beingness, which we lose when the mind gets filled with thought streaming.

We go to great lengths to recover our sense of aliveness, which we sense lies behind the screen of thought streaming. Indeed, it *is* there, but because we have such a difficult time stopping our incessant mental chatter, we use exercise, sports, and recreation to block the copious flow of thought streams. Sports enthusiasts often say that they never feel more alive than when they're completely immersed in their sport. Because of the intense focus on their specific activity, thought streaming stops. At these times, they access and feel the primal backdrop of aliveness that's there for us all. Unfortunately, thought streaming so completely obscures this aliveness that we sometimes must take dramatic measures, like skydiving or BASE-jumping, to feel it. When thought streaming is under control, we can actually feel it continuously during the day without requiring special activities or sports.

Stopping Thought Streaming Gives You an Edge

An athlete's mental attitude toward sports reflects the way he handles his mental processes during daily life. Those who encourage thought streaming in their daily affairs must also cope with it during their sports activities. Athletes who learn to stop thought streaming experience direct, often dramatic results. Those who have gained the ability to stop, slow, or control their thoughts have a definite competitive edge over their peers.

Tiger's Training in Golf

Tiger Woods' father once described a feature of his son's training before Tiger became a professional golfer. When Tiger was playing a practice round of golf and was ready to putt the ball, his father would make a sudden noise, throw an object in his son's field of sight, or otherwise try to distract him from putting. Sometimes he would drop clubs on the ground while Tiger was about to tee off, talk loudly during an approach shot, or roll an extra ball on the green as Tiger was about to putt. In all these ways, Tiger's father tried to shake his son's concentration in order to improve it. Clearly, concentrating on our thought streams keeps us distracted by altering the direction of our concentration, while disregarding these thoughts improves concentration—and sports performance.

A Clear Mind or One Streamed with Thoughts

Tiger's father was trying to improve his son's game by working on mental focus and attention. Tiger was actually learning how to increase his concentration so he could keep thought streaming under control.

Consider the thought streaming that might hamper a golfer who's ready to putt the ball in a major tournament. She may be thought streaming about her recent preparations: *"I hope that work on my swing helps get me out of this rut."* She may think about the publicity that followed a poor performance: *"Those news hounds really socked it to me when I choked in the finals last year."* She may comment on why the gallery of spectators is applauding: *"Phooey, I bet Sandy just dropped a birdie on that tough hole."* All such thoughts weaken a putter's focus and performance because a clear, open mind works best for this delicate and important part of the game.

Many golfers know intuitively that putting is best performed without thought. Actually, the best golfing in general happens when our thoughts are completely under control. I've personally worked on the mental aspects of sports with several golfers, and I've seen that a busy mind is the ultimate barrier to one's best performance. Tee shots and putting are the most problematic to a mind full of thought.

Because tee shots are much like speaking in public, thought streams about looking bad in front of a crowd frequently appear. Thought streams like this abound: *"Man, I hope I don't shank this one into the people lining the left side of the fairway. I'd have to crawl off the tee if I did that."* When golfers overcome this challenge, they typically feel the greatest satisfaction.

When I help people with the mental aspects of their golf game, we discuss what's on their mind during the session. However, I urge them to begin a long-term practice of noticing and stopping all their thought streams. Once they've gained some proficiency, when they get to the tee or green, they have more control of their mental activity and can more easily squelch distraction.

Playing Sports to Help Achieve Mental Control

On one hand, people who play sports must control their thoughts to play at high levels of achievement. On the other hand, some people actually play sports to achieve mental relief from thought streaming. Because sports activities demand so much attention if one is to play them well, they can serve as a means to stop thoughts. As the need for attention in the given sport increases, the need to stop thought streaming increases as well.

People feel great pleasure and a sense of mental relief when they manage to stop their thought streaming. Unfortunately, most sports enthusiasts need athletic activities to keep their thought streams under control. If they would practice stopping thought streaming off the field of play, they would enhance their sports activities through increased mental control. Their overall life would improve, too. Though sports enthusiasts say they like to play sports, I believe what they really mean is that they like the mental relief that sports provide. In other words, the sports activity serves as a means to an end, since many people play sports only to achieve a mental quiet that's otherwise unavailable to them.

BUSINESS AND THOUGHT STREAMING

I've been involved in some aspect of the business world since I was a young man. Our discussion about the cessation of thought streaming has particular relevance to several facets of business: Customer service, creativity, problem solving, productivity, and the quality of work.

Customer Service and Sales

Customer service and sales both have to do principally with meeting customer needs and handling difficult people. When workers have practiced stopping thought streaming, they have a consciousness that is unclouded by useless or disabling thoughts, giving them great advantage in the business world.

To actually hear what customers want from us, we first must separate ourselves from our own internal voice and preferences. Without this capability, we can't successfully respond to the needs of our customers. We end up either responding to our own needs or painting their needs according to some bias of our own. Let's say you're a customer service representative dealing with a woman's complaint, and instead of giving her your undivided attention, you engage in the following thought streaming: *"I wonder if I should change apartments. Some nice ones are being built nearby, and my child could go to a better school."* While you're interacting with the customer this way, how good or productive would your service be?

Customer service and sales professionals must also interact with difficult people who are excessively demanding or intolerant. If workers come to their jobs hindered by their own emotional baggage, they can't help being less effective in working with others. If they come to work with a clear consciousness, they'll cope better with the demands of others because they won't take what the customers say personally. Anyone who takes others' emotional outbursts personally is headed for burnout. In fact, workers whose stress results in psychological burnout have two emotional lives to cope with— their own and that of each customer.

Creativity and Problem Solving

Mental clarity is the hallmark of creativity and problem solving.

Mistakenly, some supervisors believe they are paid to worry about the performance of a company, when in truth they are paid to solve problems creatively. Worry, the condition of incessant and disturbing thoughts filling our mind, is nothing more than thought streaming on any topic of concern. When our mind is disturbed by incessant thoughts, we have no access to the open clarity required for problem solving based on creativity and insight. The solutions that come from a mind steeped in worry suffer from the limitations of perspective endemic to all forms of logical thinking.

A book I recently read on creativity in management offers an example of what I mean. Management posed the problem of how to drop an egg from a three-foot height without breaking it. The answer: raise the floor up two feet eleven inches. Although this insight isn't difficult to see, a mind filled with thought streaming would have a more difficult time coming to this solution. It gets stuck in the conceptual "box" that floors are immovable. Similarly, business managers who rely on thought streaming may apply old solutions to new problems. Can this approach be helpful to a business that wants to be competitive?

The Quality of Work

We need to stop thought streaming as a basic necessity for producing high-quality work. How can we do our best if we can't be attentive to the work at hand?

As the mind clears itself of thought streaming, we notice things that are amiss. Such flaws include a defective piece in the factory line, an inaccurately transcribed piece of data, an improperly written memo, or a poorly conceived business deal. Every business pays the price for poor-quality work. The problem nationwide has reached staggering proportions. It costs a lot of money to rework poorly made material goods, such as engines that don't work. It's also costly to repair critical errors in data, to heal the injuries of those physically hurt through inattentive driving, or to recall dangerous products such as baby toys with small, loose parts. Listen to the inner monologue of a truck driver in the throes of thought streaming: *"Hey, that's a beautiful woman over there on the sidewalk. I wonder if she's single. I'm a good driver. I can drive and look at her—no problem!"* (Crash). This kind of inattention to important details on the job has not only caused accidents, but has led to the loss of vast amounts of money in ill-conceived business deals.

If attention to other matters—a.k.a. thought streaming—dominates our consciousness, how can we properly attend to the work in front of us? We simply can't. When we see that thought streaming causes an inattention to detail, we can correct this fundamental problem and strive to produce high-quality work with our complete attention. Consistent concentration on the details of our work will ensure our success

EDUCATION AND THOUGHT STREAMING

Our educational system has the potential to train young people and many adults in the techniques and discipline required for the cessation of thought streaming. Students could receive enormous educational benefits from an increased ability to pay attention and concentrate on their studies.

Some may argue that thought streaming is good, and that a wandering mind often hits on exciting topics that thrill the imagination. Academics in particular like to cultivate a mind that ponders questions. I do, too. Yet we use the word "ponder" in very different ways. Many academics would say that thought streaming (as I use this term) and pondering are the same. As they ponder a question, they might seek to increase their mental monologue, tapping into one thought and then another. As you know by now, I don't favor this approach. I believe that the best way to ponder a problem is by reflecting on it with an open awareness that is not involved in thought streaming. During times of open awareness, I have personally had my best insights; others have as well.

At the present time, I hold a different view from academics, who believe that actively generating thought streaming is helpful. The public is only now beginning to understand that thought streaming is a different mental process from logical thinking or the single occurrence of a thought. Many people have not had adequate time to digest this new understanding fully. As people better understand the mechanics of thought, they will clearly see the mind clouded by thought streaming for the detriment that it truly is.

The Ability to Pay Attention

A fundamental requirement of a good education is the ability to pay attention. Without the ability to focus one's attention on the subject matter, learning becomes increasingly difficult. This universal point applies not only to every academic subject, but also to the vocation one is preparing for.

I believe the educational system should propagate the understanding that the encouragement of thought streaming is detrimental. Methods exist to practice dropping our fascination with it. If we taught students how thought streaming inappropriately captures their attention and diverts it from more useful tasks, and if we showed them how to decrease their preoccupation with it, we would greatly enhance the lives of our students.

Consider how you might have lived your life if, at a young age, you had been informed about thought streaming and how to control it. How different would your life have been? Most likely you would have experienced much more peace and openness.

Grade and High School Training in the Stopping of Thought Streaming

Formal training in understanding and stopping thought streaming might best begin in elementary school, perhaps in the sixth grade. (Wouldn't this make a great topic for a research project?) At this time, preteens, who are conscious of their mental activities, have enough mental capability and energy to slow or stop thought streaming. I would then recommend brief reintroductions to the exercise of stopping thought streaming during one class in each successive year. Instructors could reserve the first ten minutes of every English or science class for the practice of stopping thought streaming.

Regular practice would help enhance student's mental clarity, improve their attention, and increase their reading comprehension. Formal training would also decrease test anxiety. Since all anxiety is related to incessant, distressing thoughts, as children gained improved control over their bothersome, disturbing thought streaming, test anxiety would lessen and their scores would improve. Regular discipline in controlling thought streaming also sets the stage for consistent practice later in life, leading to enhanced mental clarity and personal effectiveness.

University Training

Within a university setting, I recommend that a philosophy class be instituted to focus on creativity, the generation of insights, and the cessation of thought streaming. The class syllabus might consist of an introduction to thinking, logical thought, thought streaming, insight, creativity, and practice in the stopping of thought streaming. Fifteen minutes of each fifty-minute class period might be dedicated to the actual practice of noticing and stopping thought streaming.

I also recommend that a class be developed specifically to aid students in the cessation of thought streaming. Like other three-credit classes, it would meet three times a week for an hour. The first 10 minutes of each class would be devoted to discussing the nature of thought streaming and the particular needs of students, such as enhancing the need for creativity because a new art project has been assigned or focusing the mind to assimilate information for an upcoming test. The remaining classroom period might include the practice of "Notice and Stop" (a form of stopping thought streaming). At the instructor's discretion, students might also learn to extend their practice while walking or sitting quietly.

Students need such a class because there are many stressors at school. Besides the worry about tests, peer pressure and violence exist. Often schools apply physical measures to avoid violence, like metal detectors and body searches. However, we can't search through the mind of someone intent on harm, yet this destructive impulse has its origin there.

Earlier I described the process of a woman who killed her children and spouse. I believe that children who express violence at school go through a similar process. Let's say that Joey is on the receiving end of insults and bullying ("Joey is a nerd! Joey is a nerd! Joey is a nerd!") The boy's thought streaming magnifies his perception of the wrong he has suffered: *"I'm not a nerd. Why are they saying that? I'm not a nerd. Now they're telling all my neighbors that, too. I'm not a nerd. I bet they're saying that in front of my girlfriend, too. They're ruining my life, spreading all these lies!"*

Joey's thought streams also focuses mental content exclusively on his suffering: *"I hate them. I can't stand that they're lying like this. I hate them. I hate them. I'll show them. I have friends. We'll show them that they can't spread lies and get away with it. We'll show them. They're still spreading lies. Everything they say is lies. They better be stopped."*

A class in the cessation of thought streaming would help Joey and thousands of other youngsters through the turbulent years of junior high and high school. Our school years are transformative, both physically and mentally. Apart from trying to teach children to do good and correct misbehavior, we don't specifically address the issue of thought streaming in any systematic way. We let our thought streams and our children's thought streams run loose, and we typically correct the behavior originating from it when it's obviously bad, involving fighting and breaking things. If we taught that thought streaming exists, that we can place it under voluntary control, and that life without thought streaming brings a greater sense of well-being, we could begin addressing many of the fundamental problems that plague our school systems.

TRY THIS:

T H E R E is a business management technique called Management By Walking Around (MBWA) in which managers walk around the home, office, school, or plant to see whether everything is working well or whether there are any problems to be solved. I suggest a new management technique called MBWA2, or management by walking around *twice*.

I N your first walk around the building or house, gather your attention by placing your focus on your thought streams and stop those that you can.

O N the second trip around the house or building, attend to your usual routine of checking up on things. Having cleared up much of your thought streaming during the first walk around, you'll deal with the problems you encounter with greater insight and clarity.

CHAPTER ELEVEN

How to Stop Thought Streaming

"You've got to do your own growing, no matter how
tall your grandfather was."
—Irish Proverb

YOU'VE traveled this far with me, so I know that you're interested in the issue of thought streaming—stopping it, preventing it, and enjoying a vastly improved life. To understand thought streaming, each of us has to recognize it in ourselves and come to a conclusion about its value. We need to determine whether we're bothered by our thought streaming or actually feel it's an aid to us. If you consider it valuable, you'll keep doing it. Please keep as much thought streaming as suits your situation; you know best for yourself. However, please hear me when I say that the more you avoid encouraging thoughts, the easier and truer your life will become.

If you've given this issue careful consideration and you've decided to explore the benefits of stopping your obsessive thinking, I'll now explore with you the methodology you'll need to make progress.

THE METHODS

How you react to each new occurrence of thought will decide both if and how you will manage your mind. If you've decided that indeed all thought streaming is harmful and choose to stop, you'll need to experiment with a few key ways to do it.

First, try to stop or disengage from all your unnecessary thoughts right now by treating them as meaningless. You've already been practicing this if you attempted the "Try this" exercises at the end of each chapter. In this first and most important method, stop or disengage from all streaming thoughts now, as well as those that arise in the future, by giving up your fascination with thought streaming of any kind. While this method appears daunting to most people, I encourage giving it your best shot anyway. Whether you use it as a method or as a goal, just use it.

Secondly, if you can't stop or disengage from your thought streaming, I recommend backing up a step. Take some time to determine how much of your waking life is actually spent thought streaming. Use this time to look at your thoughts. You can also use this time to reflect on the differences among logical thinking, individual occurrences of thought, and thought streaming.

In this approach, you simply look *at* your thoughts instead of looking *into* them. Don't attempt to figure them out. To do this, you mentally need to break away from being immersed in your thoughts. Look to see how often they occur in your life and how much repetition they involve. Look to see how many are truly logical and how many have the possibility for harm.

While it's difficult to tell someone how to look at thoughts, the process essentially involves a shift in perspective. It's like looking through dirty eyeglasses. We can wear our glasses all day and not notice how dirty they are. Yet if we take them off and examine them, we'll see that they're a mess. If we put them on again without cleaning them, we'll see the dirt we didn't see before. Basically, we've shifted our attention from a distant view to a close-up one. We can either look at the distorted scene in front of us, or we can look at the dirt on the glasses. In many ways, the dirt resembles the screen of thoughts that cloud our vision. We can look *into* the view by seeing past the dirt on our glasses, although somehow it obscures our vision, or we can change focus and look *at* the dirt. Similarly, we can *look* into the meaning of our thoughts, or we can look *at* the fact that they're present.

In my own life, I've found that my mind wants to be abuzz with thought streaming (that takes extra effort to control) when I'm in the shower. I don't know why this is so, but it's rather dramatic. I start the water, wait for it to warm up, and step in. Then— zoom!— off my mind goes, if I let it, into a barrage of thought streaming.

Sometimes when I'm driving my car, only a few thoughts creep in. Involved as I am in the simple fact of driving the car, I experience a few individual thoughts now and then. When I first noticed this lack of thought while driving, I felt encouraged. It meant that I could function clearly and efficiently without thought streaming. I didn't believe it initially but have now found it to be perfectly true.

At this point, I think it's appropriate to mention something about the exercise of watching thoughts and thought streams. In your early attempts, you probably won't have sustained awareness in watching individual thoughts. Sometimes you'll watch a few thoughts and streams of thoughts as if you were outside them looking in. Other times you won't have any distance from them at all; you'll feel completely immersed in thought streaming. Don't worry about this. Just keep up this "watching method," and, as you can, also keep stopping or disengaging from any thought streams that pop up.

Simply noticing your thoughts and thought streaming is very important. Try never to go unconscious about them. You'll experience incremental success as virtually inevitable if you keep stopping or disengaging from your thought streaming. It's similar to getting better and better when you practice a sport like tennis. Remember when you first tried a new sport? You needed a lot of practice, didn't you? Stopping or disengaging from thought streams is no different, and with practice, you'll make genuine progress. Continuing practice is helpful not only for beginners, but also for those of us who usually see our thoughts as if we're inside them looking out.

TECHNICAL AID FROM A REMINDER DEVICE

You also can use a technical aid, a reminder watch, to notice how frequently you get lost in thought streaming. There are many good brands on the market. I have used a Watch Minder™ and found it satisfactory, although I'm not endorsing this particular product. When using such a watch, you set it to vibrate or ring randomly during the day, say between 8 a.m. and 5 p.m. Many watches can be set to vibrate as often as twice each hour.

When the watch goes off, you stop and assess the state of your mind. Is it engaged in attention or logical thinking, or has it become lost in thought streaming? Let's say that you set the watch to vibrate twice an hour for eight hours. This means that sixteen times a day you'll have an opportunity to assess your mental condition and determine whether it's in a helpful state. If you notice that it's not in a helpful state, you have the opportunity to pull yourself out of any negativity.

If you use a reminder device for a while, you'll gain an appreciation for how many times a day you get lost in thought streaming. If you find that you're lost in thought for twelve of the sixteen times that the watch vibrates, you'll know that *most* of your mental life is preoccupied and unavailable for other activities or people. If you find that you're lost in thought for six of the sixteen times the reminder device vibrates, you'll know that *much* of your mental life is preoccupied and unavailable for other activities or people. If you find yourself lost in thought two times or less out of the sixteen possible times that the watch vibrates, you'll know that most of your mental life is free and available to be directed to activities, other people, or quietude.

An Exercise for Perpetuity

Whether you're out and about or at home, always be aware of your thoughts. Look at them. Whenever you notice you've gone into a thought stream, discourage it from continuing. Do this for each one that occurs.

How we actually disengage from or stop each thought stream is quite a mystery. While I know many people interested in this subject, I don't believe anyone actually knows how it happens. Yet we do have some control over stopping thought streams from continuing. Perhaps we use a mental "muscle" of some sort. We exercise that "muscle" by stopping our thoughts when we want to fall asleep at night.

If you don't care to use a technical device, you can still benefit by becoming more familiar with thought streaming. As you grow increasingly familiar with your thought patterns, remember to keep trying to discourage or stop any streaming that occurs. The following exercise will help you do this. You can use this exercise in conjunction with your reminder device or without using an aid.

Begin the exercise by sitting quietly for ten minutes and simply watching your thoughts. The method, called "Notice and Stop" is as follows:

1. *Notice* each time that you become involved in a thought stream.

2. *Stop* the thought streaming any way you can. If you can't stop it immediately, keep trying every means you know (see A, B, and C below) until the thought stream significantly diminishes or goes away completely (see A, B, and C below).

   A. Distract or disengage yourself with an activity.

   B. Drop your fascination with the thought stream by turning your attention to something else (watch a movie, attentively watch a beautiful view or scene, crochet, sweep the floor, do a puzzle, or listen carefully to someone).

   C. Concentrate your attention on a word or on your breath. For example, focus the mind repeatedly on a neutral word like "one" and repeat it internally, or count your outbreaths until you get to 10 and start back at one again.

At the end of ten minutes, stop and assess your mental processes. Did thought streaming diminish in volume and intensity or not? Did you stop or disengage from as many thought streams as you could? Great! That's all there is to it. You're on your way to decreasing worry in your life and living with greater joy.

If your thought streaming strikes you as harmful in some way (too emotionally charged with negativity, too "me"-oriented, or too judgmental), consider undertaking a long-term practice of "Notice and Stop." You don't need to do it formally while sitting in a chair for ten minutes. You can do it every moment of the day. Watching thought streaming and its discontinuation, day in and day out, provides noticeable gains in relieving worry and living more joyfully, so keep it up! The cessation of all thought streaming will not occur immediately; it happens when you finally have the insight into the harmfulness of it all. With diligent practice, it will probably take a number of years for virtually all thought streaming to stop. However, the incremental gains you make along the way feel great, and life with just decreased thought streaming is truly marvelous.

The Value of Practice

You can stop or disengage from all thought streaming. Even without practice, we already can stop some thought streaming before falling asleep. We have some success each night as we stop most thought streaming from continuing on. However, we also know nights in which thought streaming seems unstoppable, and we can't get to sleep. That's why we practice. As we learn to control them, we become more successful at getting to sleep even when difficult thought streams run through our mind. Won't that be a pleasure!

At times, you may actually resist using the Notice and Stop method. You may resist the "Notice" aspect because uncontrolled thought streaming temporarily provides safe harbor from the world. Sometimes we want to screen ourselves from the world by distancing ourselves from it. We may not like encountering life's darker aspects such as poverty, hunger, and cruelty. We often use television, movies, and thought streams to get away from these harsh realities of life. It takes courage to face these problems, and that's what we need to maintain mental awareness.

You may also resist the "Stop" aspect, too. Some thought streams are so captivating, in a pleasant or a painful way, that we can't immediately break free. Whether it's a fantasy about a new lover, emotional rage at our parents or children, or perplexity about finding a solution to a difficult problem, some thought streams are difficult to discourage. When facing these, we need courage to persevere under difficult circumstances. We tap into this courage through the faith we have developed from successfully stopping prior thought streaming. For example, all of us have successfully dropped one worry or another when we finally understood it didn't serve us. When thought streams are difficult to stop, remember that you can overcome each one with sincere and persistent effort.

OTHER AIDS

You might want to consider other aids that help stop or discourage thought streaming. First of all, noise masks thought streaming. To become aware or increase awareness of thought streams, you may need more quiet time than you're now getting. Ask for it. If someone has the television on or music is playing, ask for it to be turned down or off, or else find a more secluded place.

Secondly, activities that focus attention help you notice thought streaming. These activities include reading books, doing crossword puzzles, or participating in card games or chess. To practice awareness of thought streaming, you'll need to be attentive. Engaging in activities such as these help you remain aware of your mind's tendencies.

A DISCUSSION ON STOPPING

Again, if you believe that all your thoughts help you in daily life, feel free to continue encouraging them. Use your own experience to best indicate what you should do.

Typically, when I speak to people about stopping or disengaging from thought streaming, they're surprised by the topic at first. Most people believe that thought streaming is uncontrollable. I know for a fact that they're wrong. They're right in observing that a single instance of thought is spontaneous and uncontrollable, but they don't know that the volume of thoughts that constitutes thought streaming *can* come under voluntary control through practice.

Many people also believe initially that thought streams are so intense and intrusive that it would be too difficult to change them. They're probably only considering the goal of immediate and complete cessation of all thought, assuming this to be a valid objective. For all I know, the complete cessation of thought is impossible. However, with practice a cessation of 95 percent of thought streaming is highly likely. In addition, people experience mental relief when even 50 percent of thought streams vanish. When 95 percent of thought streaming is gone, the 5 percent that remains actually becomes barely noticeable and stops being bothersome.

If you have only a vague sense that thoughts are getting in the way of your optimal functioning, please re-read the "Notice and Stop" exercise and examine when and how often thoughts intrude into your mental landscape. Take some time to consider the impact of thought streaming on your quality of life. If you see your life experience beginning to decrease in quality because of thought streaming, you may wish to regularly practice the exercise. Do it in ways appropriate to your own life circumstances.

Because all this is probably new territory for you, you may need to take some time to assess the value of the practice versus the harm produced by thought streaming. Some of us consider it challenging to consider a life with minimal mental chatter. We wonder what it would be like, and we may fear that problems could result from trying to tamper with our mental processes.

Embrace a New Life

If this is where you find yourself, take time to consider a new life, thoroughly imbued with peace of mind and as much volitional, logical thinking as you choose. When you examine your life, can you identify any times when your thoughts take a break? Do you find that state peaceful? How much of your time is spent like this? Would you like more?

Paying attention is the key. Attention *on* your thoughts facilitates success in not following thought streams. Attention *to* your thoughts gets you involved in their content and only encourages more of them. I urge you to step out of your thoughts and to look *at* them, not *into* them. The more aware you are of them, the more success you'll have in stopping them. As you enjoy increased mental clarity and attentiveness, your life will be easier than ever before.

Sometimes in the early stages of paying attention to thought streaming, despite our best intentions, we can't immediately stop or disengage from thoughts with great success. However, with continued interest and effort, everyone can stop or disengage from virtually all of them. Success depends on maintaining a permanent commitment to stopping or disengaging from them. If you make this commitment—and it's challenging, to be sure— you'll inevitably succeed.

THE METHOD FOR MENTAL MATURITY (MMM)

Two methods greatly help us understand our mental life, grow into mental maturity, and increase our overall well-being. I discussed both of them earlier in the book. Used in conjunction with one another, they form the basis for the Method for Mental Maturity (MMM).

The first method, Notice and Stop, involves being aware of and stopping all thought streaming that enters or exists in your mind at every moment. This method clears out all harmful thought streaming and opens the door to mental clarity and insight. The second method, Root Therapy, focuses on asking yourself the question, "*And what's so bad about this?*" When you encounter a significant life problem, you keep repeating the question over and over again in an iterative fashion until you encounter the most fundamental, emotionally charged aspect of the problem (usually a firmly held belief or concept). At this point, you can subject the belief or concept to reflection and honestly examine it for its truth.

Using Root Therapy, you'll more easily find answers to difficult problems. This method works extremely well if you practice Notice and Stop for a sufficient length of time. When consistently applied, the practice of Notice and Stop results in enhanced mental clarity and supports reflection on a problem when you're involved in Root Therapy. Used together, both approaches offer us a better understanding of our problems, as well as a way to deal with others that arise.

Try This:

N O W it's time to consider the goal of ALWAYS noticing your thought streaming and ALWAYS either stopping it, discouraging it, or disengaging from it.

Y O U can do Notice and Stop with others. For encouragement, you might consider getting together with friends at your house, school, or church.

Y O U can discuss whether specific thought streams are harmful or whether morning is the best time to practice Notice and Stop. You can offer encouragement to others in the group to keep up this method of managing their mental life. You can also take time to practice Notice or both Notice and Stop together.

CHAPTER TWELVE

The Benefits of a Free Mind

"Now and then it is good to pause in our pursuit
of joy and just be joyful."
—Anonymous

W H E N we examine how thoughts link up with various thought streaming styles (such as planning, critiquing, wondering, or fantasizing), we often find the results surprising. We discover how we've mistakenly accepted a variety of detrimental activities as fundamental requirements of living.

Many examples abound about how conceptualizations have run amok and have been turned by thought streaming into harmful belief systems. Consider the religious cults created and destroyed by Jim Jones and Shoko Asahara; the political justifications for the genocidal action of the Turks against the Armenians, the Hutus against the Tutsis, and the Nazis against the Jews; the narco-materialism of a Pablo Escobar; the personal power grabs behind every political dictator; the circumscribed illogic of any pedophile; the government and police activities of South Africa in the 1980s; and all the religious persecution, intolerance, and self-righteousness throughout the ages. On a personal level, our thought streams inappropriately solidify false beliefs of worthlessness, need for control, self-hatred, and fear of failure into painful, harmful experiences.

When thought streaming creates monolithic belief systems, with power centralized in a charismatic personality, great potential for harm exists. Thought streaming then leaves no room for questioning, no ability to ask whether sanctioned activities are appropriate and helpful on a larger scale.

In general, it's hard to know whether our thought streaming is reality-based or whether it's a distortion of true facts. In any event, we would do better to stop the thought streaming in our own mind. When it has ceased, we'll have the clarity to understand situations more fully and the wisdom to act in the best interests of all.

STOPPING THOUGHT STREAMS

In the examples I've just given, I've tried to expose the dangers of a mental process that occurs unwittingly in all of us. We don't ordinarily understand how damaging thought streaming is to ourselves and others.

Thought streaming offers us little in the way of lasting benefits. It may help us get through times of sheer boredom in our life. It may offer us harmless entertainment when we raise "what-if" scenarios that delve into one unfathomable interpersonal mystery after another or into some possible hidden cause of our bad luck. However, with thought streaming we always pay a hidden price.

Unfortunately, we don't have to expend a lot of energy to play host to thought streams. They start automatically with the appearance of every initial thought. So we need to be vigilant and remember the harm they cause. We need to stop our fascination with where we believe they'll lead us. Otherwise, thought streams will take us down the wrong, harmful road.

Without a doubt, thought streaming diverts our attention from important matters and keeps us from living fully and openly. Thought streaming separates us from others who hold different views, making them appear as enemies instead of colleagues whose diverse opinions have equal validity with our own in contributing to the greater community. The separation that results from thought streaming also fosters self-righteousness, which is detrimental to free and open discussion of issues. Finally, thought streaming can take us to illogical conclusions and encourage us to act on these falsehoods. In this regard, the most harmful thought streams limit our own views of ourselves. I don't know a worse way to live one's life than this.

AFTER STOPPING THOUGHT STREAMS

I've devoted much of this book to a discussion of thought streaming. Now I'd like to describe what life is like *without* thought streaming. It isn't easy for most of us to comprehend how that would be. From my own personal experience as well as the experiences others report to me, I can say that life becomes simple, mentally easy and attentive, and joyous.

To begin with, falling asleep is as easy as falling off a log. Thought streaming doesn't captivate my attention and keep me from dropping right off each night. How is it for you? I also experience a new way of waking up. In the morning, when I decide whether I should get right up or whether I should continue sleeping, I look at my thought. If it's trying to start a streaming mode, I know that I'm awake and ready for the day. If I notice that the energy of thought streaming is low, I need to roll over and get a few more winks.

When thought streaming has virtually ceased, individual thoughts still come into one's consciousness. They always have and always will. We wouldn't want to completely stop individual thoughts because where would we be without logic, insight, and inspiration? However, we certainly want to shut down continuous thought streaming, especially when we have acquired a taste for clarity.

I'll now try to convey a sense of how the mind operates when thought streaming is under control. I offer this example from my own personal experience.

Once a new thought occurs (let's say it's about a needed repair to the house), I either attend to it or not as a voluntary choice. If the thought is noticed, I voluntarily consider it. I may think, *"Hmm, the house needs a repair; let me look into that."* If the thought is dismissed, it passes away without much attention directed to it and disappears completely and immediately from consciousness.

If I've attended to the thought, I look into the issue consciously and logically: *"The room needs paint, and some of the walls need holes repaired. I'll get the paint and spackle on Friday and start the work Saturday morning."* When I've completed the logical thinking process, the topic comes to an end, with no thoughts that linger about those wall repairs. On Friday, no "reminder" thought streaming arises about getting to the store to buy supplies. I do get to the store as planned, but by knowing, not by thought streaming myself into submission to do so.

Of course, thoughts on other topics will arise all the time, and I'll go through the same process again, either selecting or discarding the new thoughts for consideration. I handle each arising thought in the same manner. What characterizes this process is *choice:* I have the freedom to look further into each thought or disregard it as an active choice.

One of the greatest benefits of stopping thought streaming is that it frees our mind from unexamined belief systems. Thought streaming encourages beliefs by focusing on a few elements of thought and increasing our emotional attachment to it. Let's return to the example I gave before about children and obedience. The thought streaming might go like this: *"This terribly disobedient child must understand the need to behave. Where would the world be if people didn't follow rules? People should follow rules to the letter."*

By thought streaming about the belief in the meaning and value of obedience, this person solidifies it as a construct and increases the emotional tone around the belief. In this example, we can see that anger is building in this thought streamer. Without thought streaming, the person would have no special focus on thoughts or their constructs, viewing them as one possibility among many. This openness would not cause a selective inattention to other facts, including that the "disobedient child" might have a hearing problem. Without thought streaming, the person expands the field of possibilities and doesn't get locked into inappropriate emotional responses.

When we stop thought streams, we protect ourselves from being victimized by false beliefs that we construct and maintain. We're also protected from life problems that can turn into devastating psychological states such as anxiety and depressive conditions. The seamstress, Joan, whom I discussed in a previous chapter, held the belief that she was worthless. However, that belief did not represent the truth. When Joan learned to stop thought streaming, that belief began to dissolve since it found less support in her mental monologue. She stopped telling herself that she was worthless, and she acknowledged that she was competent at her job. Her loving son moved near her, and her friends kept reinforcing that her thought streaming was false. All these positive inputs dramatically weakened the thought streaming that supported her belief in her worthlessness. Her belief just didn't fit with reality.

No More Time Needed to Collect One's Thoughts

Have you heard people say that they need time to collect their thoughts? In terms of thought streaming, this means two things. First, their thought streams are running rampant, and they need a moment or two to slow them down. When thought streams are spinning out of control, we need time "to reflect" or use other rational processes to help us make sense of the situation. What we're actually saying, though, is that we need time to practice an instinctual form of thought streaming control. We need to use our mental faculties for a moment, to reflect on the situation, and to determine whether we need to take action.

Secondly, when we "need time to collect our thoughts" we're acknowledging that our recent thoughts carry a significant emotional charge. Perhaps they've made us cry or feel grief-stricken. We feel emotionally overloaded. This emotional load, which originated from rapid and intense thought streaming, has prevented us from being able to think clearly. Thus we can't consider a new thought without its being corrupted by emotional overflow from the previous one. In situations like this, we sense that we should stop thought streaming, but without conscious practice, we remain at the mercy of our uncontrolled thoughts.

When you stop your thought streaming, you'll never need extra time to collect your thoughts because your mind never overloads. It will be ready and available to learn about new things.

Mental Spaciousness: More Time between Successive Thoughts

Apart from the wonderful ability to select certain thoughts as a voluntary focus of attention, you'll enjoy another unexpected benefit. As your practice improves, you'll discover that sometimes thoughts seem so uninteresting that they never even break into consciousness. If you're paying close attention, you'll notice them as incompletely formed thought fragments that pop up into consciousness but are passed over quickly, since they're not organized enough to draw attention to themselves.

As you gain mastery in stopping thought streaming, a mental spaciousness develops. What I mean by "spaciousness" is no mystery. It simply means that the time interval between successive thoughts lengthens. The time between thoughts may lengthen slowly, but with practice the process is inevitable.

Each perceived lengthening of the time interval between successive thoughts provides an increased sense of mental ease. Try to reflect on how your own life will be and feel if all your worried thought streaming completely stops. It will dramatically change your interior landscape. You'll notice how others struggle with their thought streaming, and you'll see the increased anxiety it causes them. Naturally, you'll feel compassionate toward those with intense thought streaming, since you'll remember how problematic it once made your own life.

With space between your thoughts, any emotional energy from a prior thought has time to dissipate completely before the next thought appears in your consciousness. When that next thought does come into your awareness, you can consider it with clarity, since it comes by itself and without excess emotionality or conceptualization carried over from previous thoughts.

LIFE WITHOUT THOUGHT STREAMING

I have described a life without thought streams as simple, attentive, mentally easy, and joyous. This is certainly how life becomes. When you face a problem now, how do you mentally work with it? My guess is that when the problem occurs, you have an emotional reaction and some thoughts about it. Then your thoughts intensify and stream on repetitively and harmfully. Your thought streams probably continue to examine the problem from different angles, linking one scenario to another. They consider other people's reactions and reflect on similar situations you've experienced in the past. It goes on and on, doesn't it?

This process creates a tremendous amount of needless anxiety. Yet does that additional thought streaming really help solve your problem? From personal experience, I know that it doesn't.

Imagine coming to a new problem once your thought streaming is under control. You'll have an initial emotional reaction to the situation, plus the initial thoughts, but nothing additional. No repeated and useless mental monologue will occur. Needless additional anxiety just won't happen. With a clear consciousness, you'll then chat amiably with a loved one, fully appreciate the goods available at a market, or read with complete attention the book in front of you. What a vast difference there is between a mind clouded by thought streaming and one that's completely clear and available!

What you'll appreciate most of all is the reappearance of the basic "aliveness" that you enjoy so much. It was simply clouded over when you were lost in thought. Most people go on vacation, play sports, go to the movies, knit or crochet, work crosswords, and perform a whole host of activities to regain connection to this feeling of being really alive. Even though we lose it when we're "stressed," we all know what this basic aliveness feels like. Take a moment to reflect on your personal experience of it. It feels GREAT! Why not get back to it more often? Better yet, why not always remain in contact with it? When it's within your grasp with practice, it's a pity to lose contact with it.

Early in the book, I mentioned a number of important questions I had when I began studying psychology. They stemmed from my desire to better understand courage, love, and consciousness. Many people in their 20's ask these questions but don't find answers. Yet I can say that by dropping fascination with thought streaming, I found answers to many of my questions. I've discovered that behind our thought streams lies our basic being, our basic aliveness, our basic consciousness—the wellspring that knows what to do, how to behave, and how to speak. At this level, we're free of the petty jealousies, fears, and hatreds that typically characterize our mental chatter. With thought streams gone, our fundamental intelligence offers love, knows appropriate action, and doesn't at all mind a courageous sacrifice for a higher cause. A peek behind the curtain of thought streams provides a glimpse into a better way of living and being. With thought streams gone, you'll continually experience life as a real joy.

YOUR TURN!

So now you have an opportunity to gain considerable mental relief and reestablish the link to your basic aliveness. You've had the good fortune to read about thought streaming and the negative ways it can affect your life. You also understand that thought streaming doesn't help solve any of your problems. I hope that you'll heed this advice and practice stopping thought streams as much as you can. If you continue this most worthwhile practice, you'll not only experience less chronic dissatisfaction with life, but you'll also gain more open-mindedness and mental concentration. The true joy of living will return.

I don't know how long it will take you to get significant relief from your uncontrolled thoughts. It depends on how completely you realize the destructive nature of thought streaming. As soon as you begin examining your mental life in earnest, conscientious attention initially will slow thought streaming and then eventually bring it to a halt.

Pay attention at every opportunity. It's free! You don't need special equipment; you don't have to get up unusually early or follow a certain diet. Begin by noticing your thoughts. Look *at* them, not *into* them. The more you look at them, the more you'll determine their true value. As soon as you get into the habit of noticing your thought streaming, you're on your way! Just keep noticing them and stopping them at every opportunity. Utilize a form of ceaseless practice.

I encourage you to practice noticing your thought streams and breaking away from them. If you have the intention and energy, I suggest that you form small groups to practice together and discuss your results. Groups like these can be very encouraging. I will work as I can to support you and will try to change how psychotherapists view the importance of thought streaming. The more we understand the harmfulness of thought streams, the more we'll engage life more fully and productively.

My best wishes to you.

Put down your thought streaming!

TRY THIS:

RECONSIDER the goal of noticing all your thought streaming by either stopping it, discouraging it, drawing your attention away from it, or just dropping your fascination with it.

YOU'LL find it easy to do this during your first cup of tea or coffee in the morning. It's a marvelous way to start the day. The mind is often at its quietest and most manageable the first thing in the morning, so your mental work will be easier, and you'll have greater success. During this time, simply notice your thought streaming and stop or disengage from what you can.

IF you combine a regular morning activity of stopping thought streaming with attempts to do so at other times during the day (say five minutes before the start of a meeting), you'll develop a mind that's clear of harmful disturbances.

FREE YOUR MIND

An Open Letter to the Editors of Two Psychotherapeutic Journals

Sent July 4, 2004 to:
American Psychologist (apeditor@apa.org)
American Journal of Psychiatry (apa@psych.org)

Dear Editor,

I'm writing to suggest a change in the nomenclature of the Diagnostic and Statistical Manual of Mental Disorders and the decision trees that are used for differential diagnosis. I suggest that a diagnosis related to "uncontrolled thought streaming" be created and used as a superordinate category covering all anxiety disorders.

We know that there are three types of mental processes involved in human mentation. These are logical (Aristotelian) thinking; the occurrence of individual thought (i.e., probably less than about one second in duration); and what I have termed "thought streaming," the internal mental monologue, distinct from thinking and individual thought occurrences, which takes up the rest of the internal landscape when mental silence is unavailable.

Logical thinking is a volitional, practical, and helpful process. As one of the hallmarks that differentiate us from all other species, it lies at the root of what it means to be human. Individual occurrences of thought are involuntary and are difficult to categorize as either helpful or harmful. They are what they are, and we all must cope with what comes to us through this involuntary process. Certainly, the significant insights of Watson and Crick as well as Einstein indicate that individual thoughts have been beneficial. Individual thoughts of homicide or suicide, however, are undoubtedly harmful.

Thought streaming, the process that takes up much of our mental landscape, is a volitionally maintained condition. It is a volitional process because it can be stopped (e.g., in going to sleep each night, we manage to stop it, and it stops under conditions of high attention, such as watching an interesting movie and reading music). Granted, we can't stop all thought streaming when we wish to stop it; we're aware of catchy pop songs, called "ear worms," and other subclinical obsessive thought streams. Yet all of us can stop simple thought streams, and many can stop intrusive ones that focus on self-harm, anger, and catchy song lyrics. The degree of control each of us has over our own thought streaming depends on the strength of our intention to stop them, our actual practice at stopping them, the degree of harm we perceive in them, and our inherent fascination with their content.

Overall, thought streaming poses significant harm to individuals and communities. True, the thought streaming called "daydreaming" can offer temporary relief from boredom. However, we can't always determine whether avoiding boredom or facing it head-on is the best approach.

I count at least seven types of harm that originate from thought streaming. These include (1) disturbing activities and causing anxious states of mind (such as not being able to go to sleep because of intrusive thought streaming and having thought streams of worry, even though one can do nothing to change the worrisome situation);

(2) decreasing intimacy (for example, thought streaming mentally blocks our ability to listen to others because our attention is captured by the content of the thought streaming); (3) excessive speculation (like avoiding reality by speculating on the presently unknowable); (4) inappropriate egocentricity (the majority of all thought streams are either directly or indirectly about "me"); (5) unnecessary frustration (for example, we mistakenly believe thought streaming provides answers to problems and feel frustrated when it fails to yield solutions); (6) an inappropriate focus on the thought content (clearly, the delusional drives of 20th century assassins originate from continued thought streaming that became overly focused on personal failure); and (7) the inappropriate solidifying of conceptualizations (such as stereotyping specific categories of race or gender).

Because thought streaming is a volitional process and is harmful as listed above, I suggest that it be included in the diagnostic schema for mental disorders. Where it is placed among the criteria, I leave to the expertise of your advisory panels. That thought streaming is directly related to anxiety seems certain. If there were no thought streaming related to worrying, could there be anxiety? It doesn't seem possible. Yet there are no clinically relevant generalized anxieties—phobias, OCD, PTSD, etc.—for people whose thought streaming has either stopped or is under control. Therefore, I suggest evaluating "Uncontrolled Thought Streaming" as a superordinate diagnosis over all anxiety disorders. It may hold such rank over mood disorders and others, such as hypochondriasis, but more research seems warranted before making this distinction.

Finally, since the cessation of thought streaming prevents many mental disorders, two further points need to be made. First, as a preventative measure, stopping thought streaming relates to decreases in mental illness and increases in mental health and happiness. Secondly, students in school would benefit from stopping thought streaming. If grade school curricula offered training in overcoming the harmful aspects of uncontrolled thought streaming, students would experience increased mental health and happiness throughout the rest of their lives.

Sincerely,
Steven Pashko, Ph.D.

ABOUT THE AUTHOR

STEVEN PASHKO has devoted his personal and professional life to understanding the mind, improving the quality of life, and identifying cost-effective therapies. During his long academic career, he has studied the traditional fields of biology, philosophy, pharmacology, and clinical psychology. Dr. Pashko's studies culminated in a doctorate in central nervous system pharmacology, a license in psychology, a love of poetry, and a consistent daily meditation practice. In December 1999, he had the insight of completely understanding the futility and harmfulness of allowing one's thoughts to proliferate into streams. This insight led to the full and complete resolution of the primary error of thought streaming so that thought streaming no longer captivates his attention. He uses the term "thought streaming" to help others better understand the distinction between streaming thoughts and truly useful, logical thinking.

A resident of Pennsylvania, Dr. Pashko shares his insights with others through corporate advising, seminars, public speaking, and workshops. He speaks on topics related to psychology, such as anger, anxiety/ worry, depression, personality, relationships, self-esteem, substance abuse, and well-being. He also speaks on the mental challenges of sports; business topics, such as creativity, customer service, problem solving, sales and quality of work; and education. His website is www.StevenPashko.com.

Dr. Steven Pashko is available for
advising, seminars, speaking and workshops.
He can be contacted at www.StevenPashko.com